Blanket Chests

Outstanding Designs from 30 of the World's Finest Furniture Makers

Scott Gibson and Peter Turner

The Taunton Press

THE TAUNTON PRESS, INC.
63 South Main Street, PO Box 5506, Newtown, CT 06470-5506
e-mail: tp@taunton.com

EDITOR Jennifer Renjilian Morris
COPY EDITOR Seth Reichgott
COVER DESIGN Jean-Marc Troadec
INTERIOR DESIGN Nick Caruso
LAYOUT Nick Caruso
ILLUSTRATOR Christopher Mills, except p. 27 by Rodney Diaz

Library of Congress Cataloging-in-Publication Data
Gibson, Scott, 1951-
  Blanket chests : outstanding designs from 30 of the world's finest
furniture makers / Scott Gibson and Peter Turner.
      p. cm.
  Features furniture designed by Brian Sargent and others.
  Includes index.
  ISBN 978-1-60085-299-2
  1. Chests--Design and construction. 2. Furniture making. I. Turner,
Peter, 1953- II. Sargent, Brian (Brian L.) III. Title.
  TT197.G475 2011
  684.1'6--dc22

                          2010047986

Printed in the United States of America
10 9 8 7 6 5 4 3

The following manufacturers/names appearing in *Blanket Chests* are
trademarks: Accuride®, Adobe℠, Bessey®, Feast Watson®, Festool®,
Floorseal®, General Finishes®, Lamello®, Lee Valley®, Minwax®, Multi-
Router®, Osmo®, Rockler Woodworking and Hardware℠, SOSS®,
Stabilus®, Watco®

ABOUT YOUR SAFETY
Working wood is inherently dangerous. Using hand or power tools
improperly or ignoring safety practices can lead to permanent injury
or even death. Don't try to perform operations you learn about here (or
elsewhere) unless you're certain they are safe for you. If something about
an operation doesn't feel right, don't do it. Look for another way. We
want you to enjoy the craft, so please keep safety foremost in your mind
whenever you're in the shop.

Acknowledgments

There are easier ways to make a living in a digital universe than building furniture. But as the world around us becomes more virtual and less actual, good work coming out of small shops and studios grows ever more valuable.

And that is what we have here: 30 pieces by 30 artisans who have combined manual and artistic skills to produce objects of beauty as well as practicality. We gratefully acknowledge their willingness to share what they do.

A number of craftsmen represented in this book went out of their way to demonstrate particular techniques important to their work. Thank you Craig Thibodeau, Darrell Peart, Mitch Ryerson, Michael Cullen, Brian Sargent, Shona Kinniburgh, and Tim Whitten.

A special thank you to Ann Scheid with the Greene and Greene Archives at the University of Southern California for helping us track down a rare image of a Greene and Greene chest important to Darrell Peart's work.

Thanks also to Carolyn Mandarano, Jennifer Renjilian Morris, Lucy Handley, Katy Binder, our illustrator Christopher Mills, our copy editor Seth Reichgott, and the entire design and production department at The Taunton Press for their usual attention to detail and their commitment to getting it right. Thanks also go to Helen Albert for her early support of this project.

Finally, we're grateful for the support of our families. Thank you Susan and Colleen, Morrigan, Emily, Benjamin, and Molly.

Contents

Introduction

Chests are a very old form of furniture, used over thousands of years to store everything from wedding dowries to woolen blankets, table linens to winter sweaters. Although each chest is basically a box with a lid, craftsmen have been unusually inventive in tailoring this fundamental piece of furniture to the style and needs of their times.

This book contains 30 chests in styles that span at least 300 years and probably longer. There are a number of traditional period pieces; if not exact reproductions of early American and European chests, then they are at least heavily indebted to them. You'll also find several strikingly contemporary pieces and a number that combine elements of old and new.

Many of the artisans here are from the United States, with a natural inclination toward American furniture forms. But we also have representation from Europe, Canada, and even Australia. With this depth of talent it is no surprise to see there are many ways of elevating what might be just a box into something entirely different.

For all of this diversity, construction techniques are straightforward, proven, and reliable. To that end, we have included a chapter at the beginning of the book—Chest-Building Techniques—that describes the essentials of joinery that might be used on any chest. As you continue through the book, you'll find with each chest a brief design explanation that addresses what the artisan had in mind, although not necessarily a description of how the chest was built. The accompanying drawings provide those details.

The work here demonstrates that a furniture form is only a starting point. If storage were the only aim, we could all use cardboard bankers' boxes. Thankfully, that's not the case.

CHEST-BUILDING TECHNIQUES

Blanket chests are functional pieces of furniture, and for all of their variety in design, materials, and surface decoration, they rely on fundamental case joinery for strength and durability. At its simplest, a blanket chest is six boards, four of them nailed at the corners to form the case and the other two used for the top and bottom. But joinery is often more elaborate and more durable. Many chests are assembled with variations on three basic woodworking joints: mortises and tenons, dovetails, and miters.

Each technique offers tremendous flexibility, not only in how the joints are made but also in how they are put to use. A mortise-and-tenon joint, for example, can be formed with a router, a hollow-chisel mortising machine and a tablesaw, or entirely with hand tools. This basic joint is the foundation of frame-and-panel construction for chest sides, bottoms, and tops.

Dovetails come in just as many forms. They can be made with a few simple hand tools—a saw, a chisel or two and a mallet, a marking knife—or produced in minutes with one of many commercially made router jigs. No matter how they are executed, dovetails can join case sides, bases, and drawers with an unrivaled combination of strength and elegance.

Carcase miters can be cut on a tablesaw, router table, or shaper. They can be reinforced using keys, splines, biscuits, or glue blocks.

There are certainly other approaches. Rabbets, dowel joints, biscuit joinery (and its cousin, the proprietary Domino joinery from Festool®), box joints, and even nailed or screwed butt joints all are options for assembling a chest or some of its components. But dovetail and mortise-and-tenon joints are bedrock woodworking techniques for the kind of casework you'll see here. Very often the choice of joinery comes down to experience and aesthetics.

This chapter is an abbreviated guide to a few construction techniques useful for building chests. More specialized techniques specific to individual chests are explained, where appropriate, in the chapters that follow.

Mortises

One thing that makes a mortise-and-tenon joint so useful is its versatility, but in all of its forms, it's fairly simple: a recess cut into one piece of stock (the mortise) and a corresponding male part (the tenon) in the other. Although they're typically used for right-angle connections, a mortise-and-tenon joint also can be adapted for angled components.

Mortises can be cut in one of several ways: with a plunge router, which produces a slot with rounded ends; with a mortising machine, which makes a square-shouldered slot; with a drill press; or even by hand with a drill, a chisel, and a mallet if you have the time and patience. The object is to produce a mortise with smooth walls for good glue adhesion and uniform dimensions.

Tools used to make mortises, such as router bits or hollow chisels, generally aren't adjustable. So cut the mortise first, then make trial-and-error adjustments to the tenon for a good fit, which is crucial to the strength of the joint.

Cutting mortises with a plunge router

1. Two fences keep the router on track when cutting a mortise. One rides along the outside of the workpiece, adjusted to position the bit over the mortise. The other, attached to the base plate of the router with double-sided tape, prevents the router from twisting and tilting.

2. Make a number of passes, removing a little material each time. A ¼-in. carbide spiral bit plunges into the surface easily and makes a smooth cut. A second piece of material clamped next to the workpiece helps keep the router stable by providing a larger work surface.

3. The bit leaves each end of the mortise with rounded corners. If the matching tenon will be machined with square shoulders, square up the mortise with a chisel.

4. The finished mortise also can be left with rounded corners. In this case, round the ends of the tenon to match it. There's no structural advantage to either approach.

Cutting mortises by hand

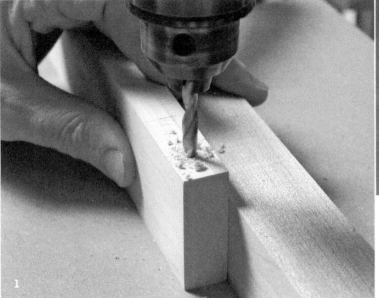

1. Start by laying out the mortise on the edge of the workpiece and set up the drill press fence so the bit engages the work correctly. Drill holes 1/8-in. from the layout lines at each end of the mortise, then drill as many intermediate holes as necessary.

2. Clean up the mortise with chisels. A mortising chisel of the correct width makes a clean cross-grain cut at the end of the mortise. A wider paring chisel cleans up the walls of the mortise.

Cutting mortises with a hollow-chisel mortising machine

1. Lay out the location of the mortise on a test piece of the same thickness as the workpiece. Lower the bit (with the machine turned off), adjust the fence to line up the edge of the bit with the layout mark, and then make a test plunge.

2. Keep adjusting the fence and making test holes until the mortise is exactly centered in the stock. Then switch to the workpiece and make a series of overlapping holes to create the mortise.

3. Some debris will probably have to be cleared from the mortise, but it otherwise is complete. The mortise should be dead center in the middle of the workpiece.

Tenons

Tenons can be cut separately on a tablesaw and inserted into corresponding mortises (these are called floating tenons) or milled into the end of a piece of stock with one of several techniques.

Mortise-and-tenon joints get their superior strength from a good fit and a strong glue bond, as well as from the shoulders of the tenon, which help prevent racking and distortion. Ideally, the tenon will slide into the mortise with some resistance but not enough to require a clamp or a hammer for persuasion. That said, machining slightly oversize tenons is better than making undersize ones because they can be trimmed with a shoulder plane for a perfect fit.

Tenons can be formed with a fine-tooth saw, with a dado on the tablesaw, with a tablesaw tenoning jig, with a bandsaw, or on a specialized router tool like the Multi-Router®. Once a machine has been set up to make a tenon accurately, many can be run off in very little time. Work with test pieces the exact same thickness as the workpiece and take your time. Once the tenon fits correctly, run off another test piece to make sure and then have at it.

Cutting tenons by hand

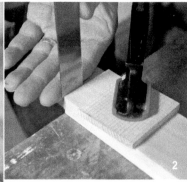

1. After laying out the tenon, make the shoulder cuts first. Then put the workpiece in a vise and cut down along the layout line. Try to split the line with the sawblade on the waste side, but don't wander inside the line.

2 & 3. Use a chisel to clean up the shoulders, paring to the knife line. For the final cut, place the blade of the chisel in the scribe line created by a marking gauge or knife and press down firmly. Keep the chisel perpendicular to the work.

Cutting tenons on a tablesaw

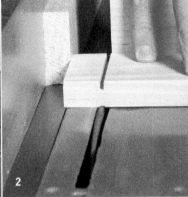

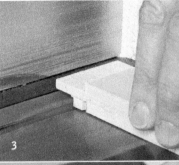

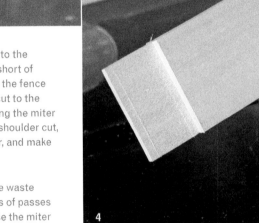

1. Lay out the tenon on the end of the workpiece by scribing a baseline and lines for the two cheeks. Filling in the scribed marks with pencil makes them easier to see. Now set the height of the blade so it just kisses the layout line.

2. Clamp a board to the fence so it stops short of the blade, and set the fence so the blade will cut to the shoulder line. Using the miter gauge, make one shoulder cut, flip the board over, and make the other.

3. Nibble away the waste by making a series of passes over the blade. Use the miter gauge and hold the work firmly for each pass. When one side is finished, flip the board over and do the other side.

4. The tablesaw should make a smooth face with only minor ridges. These can be cleaned up with a shoulder plane when the tenon is complete.

5. If the tenon is to have a shoulder at top and bottom, use the same fence setting on the tablesaw to make a clean cut at the shoulder. The ears of the tenon can be removed with a handsaw and cleaned up with a chisel.

Cutting tenons with a tablesaw jig

1. A commercial tenoning jig clamps the work securely while the cheek cuts are made. Shoulder cuts are made with a miter gauge and fence first, just as they would be if making the tenons with a tablesaw blade alone.

2. Any ridges or irregularities the tablesaw blade leaves behind can be removed with a chisel.

Frame-and-Panel Construction

There are numerous examples of chests in this book made at least in part with frame-and-panel assemblies. It's one of the most useful construction techniques in woodworking because it can be applied to so many situations. Unlike solid lumber, frame-and-panel components shrink and swell very little with changes in relative humidity because the panels are isolated from the frame pieces.

Frames are put together with mortise-and-tenon joints. Rails and stiles get a groove on the inside edge to accommodate the panels. For connections where strength is important (at the corners of the assembly, for instance), tenons are longer than the groove is deep, so additional mortises are cut at the bottom of the groove. The corresponding tenon gets a notch, called a haunch, to fill the groove. For intermediate locations where strength isn't as much of an issue, a shorter tenon engages only the panel groove. That's called a stub tenon.

Panels should be sized so there's a little space between the edge and the bottom of the groove. The wider the panel, the more wiggle room it needs (for more on wood movement, see p. 26). This gives the panel a place to expand when humidity is high without damaging the frame.

Unless they're made from plywood, panels aren't glued all the way around the frames. They can, however, be pinned or glued at the center point of the ends to keep them from shifting in their openings. The wood will still be able to move seasonally on either side of the pin. Some furniture makers use small-diameter wood pins to secure the panels, first drilling a pilot hole slightly smaller than the pin and then tapping the pin home with a spot of glue on the end. Others use brads. Just clip off the head of the nail, drill a pilot hole, and tape the pin in. Be sure it's not long enough to pop out the other side. Or, you can just use a small air nail.

Frame-and-panel assembly

1. A router table is a convenient way to make the grooves on the inside faces of the stiles and rails. The groove is cut the full length of each piece. The same bit can be used for both the groove and the deeper mortises.

2. Because the groove is typically only 1/2 in. deep, deepening it for a full mortise-and-tenon assembly will provide more glue surface and make the finished frame stronger. The mortise can be machined with a plunge router.

3. The corresponding tenon gets a haunch at one end that fills the ends of the groove.

4. Cut flat panels on a tablesaw, first by making the shoulder cut with the panel flat on the saw, then finishing the tongue by running the panel past the blade on edge. The panel should be sized so there is room for it to shrink and expand seasonally in the frame.

5. The panel should slide easily into the grooves in the rails and stiles. Dry-fit all the pieces and make any necessary adjustments before applying any glue.

6. When gluing up the assembly, be careful to apply glue so it won't ooze into the grooves and grab the panel.

7. Secure the panel with a single pin in the middle of the panel top and bottom. This keeps the panel centered in the frame with an even reveal all around while still allowing seasonal movement. A toothpick makes a good pin.

Breadboard Ends

Breadboard ends, which help keep solid pieces of lumber flat, are cross-grain battens, or breadboards, that are affixed to both ends of a solid wood panel. The strongest and most durable method of attaching breadboards is to make a few mortises and tenons in conjunction with a continuous short tongue and a mating groove. The deep tenons support the battens while the shallow tongue and groove keep the panel and its ends in alignment.

Typically, a breadboard is glued only at the center point to allow for cross-grain movement in the panel. Farther away from the center, mortises must provide space for the tenons to move as the panel comes and goes with seasonal moisture changes. Holes for pins in the tenons must be elongated to prevent the pins from restricting the panel.

Some furniture makers stop the groove in the batten before the end of the board so the groove can't be seen when the breadboard is attached (that's how Peter Turner is making the one shown here). Others run the groove all the way through. It's really a matter of personal preference.

One trick for getting a very tight fit at the joint between the panel and the batten is to take a few passes with a hand plane on the edge of the batten near its center. This creates a very small belly in the joint. When it's clamped tight there, the ends of the batten will be less likely to show a gap.

Frame-and-panel assembly

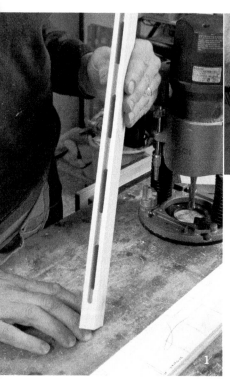

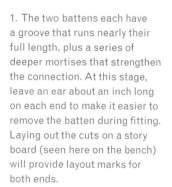

1. The two battens each have a groove that runs nearly their full length, plus a series of deeper mortises that strengthen the connection. At this stage, leave an ear about an inch long on each end to make it easier to remove the batten during fitting. Laying out the cuts on a story board (seen here on the bench) will provide layout marks for both ends.

2. Lay out the tongue and tenons on the end of the top, making sure to continue the marks across the end for later reference. Then use a router to remove most of the waste. For now, leave material between the tenons to support the router base during the cut. Set the depth of cut on a scrap of wood the same thickness as the workpiece.

3. Mark the edges of the tenons and the baseline. The router may have obliterated the original layout marks but the lines on the end of the piece will allow them to be re-established. A scrap slightly narrower than the groove in the batten makes a convenient gauge for establishing the baseline.

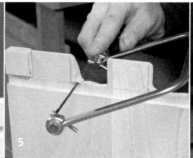

5. Remove waste between tenons with a coping saw.

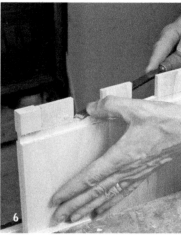

4. With a fine-tooth saw, cut down to the baseline to establish the edges of each tenon.

6. Now pare to the baseline with a chisel. The finished tongue must be slightly shorter than the depth of the groove in the batten.

7. Test-fit the batten on the end of the top and make any necessary adjustments. Then remove the batten and drill holes for the pins all the way through at the center of each tenon location. Reassemble the pieces, mark the hole locations on the tenons, and drill holes for the pins. Holes on the outside tenons may be set slightly toward the shoulder so the batten will snug up tightly to the top. This is called a drawbore.

8. Holes on the outside tenons should be elongated to allow the top to shrink and expand seasonally. Drill two holes a slight distance apart and use a chisel to clean out the material between them.

9. Now it's time to test fit the two. The batten should fit snugly. Mark the edges of the top on the batten and cut off the ears.

10. Apply some glue to the center tenons only and clamp the pieces together. Then tap the pins home.

Through Dovetails

Through dovetails are a classic joint for blanket chests. Their width and spacing can be adjusted to suit the maker's taste. This joint is made with a series of interlocking tapered pieces called pins and tails that form a strong and attractive connection.

There are a variety of ways to make this joint. The simplest method is by hand, with rip and crosscut saws (or a Japanese-style saw), a few chisels, and a mallet. One side of the joint is sawn and pared, then used to lay out the second side. If the cuts are accurate, the joint slides snugly together and any pins or tails that protrude are trimmed flat with a handplane.

Some cabinetmakers start with the pins and use those to lay out the corresponding tails. The approach illustrated here is tails first.

There also are various ways to use power tools to cut this joint; commercial router jigs are probably the most common, and using one makes sense when the objective is to make a stack of kitchen drawers. Making dovetails by hand is slower, but it's a much more flexible approach where pin spacing and width is entirely up to the maker.

Cutting through dovetails

1. Start by scribing a baseline on both faces of the workpiece for the tails. The distance from the end of the board to this line should be just slightly more than the thickness of the board in which the pins will be cut.

2. With a marking knife, continue the baselines across both edges. The end of the board should now have a continuous scribe line the same distance from the end.

3. Lay out the tails with an adjustable bevel. The angle for hardwoods is typically set at 1:8; for softwoods it's usually 1:6.

4. Mark the areas to be removed with a colored pencil to help minimize mistakes.

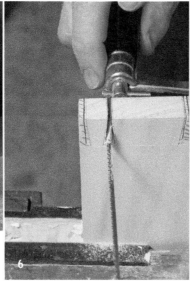

5. Cut on the waste side of the line all the way to the baseline, but be careful not to go past it. If these cuts are not flat and square, they will have to be pared back to the line with a chisel.

6. Most of the waste can be removed with a coping saw, but the cut should stay safely away from the baseline and the scribe lines for the tails.

7. Working carefully, pare to the line with a chisel. The object is to get a clean, straight face on each tail surface and to keep the faces uniformly square to the face of the board. Waste above the baseline also should be pared away with a chisel.

8. Use the tail piece to lay out the pins. The pin board also gets scribed baselines. A lead holder gets into very tight spaces without hitting adjacent faces.

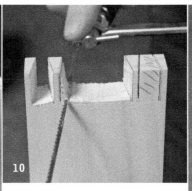

9. Mark the area to be removed with a colored pencil and saw to the layout lines on the waste side.

10. Remove the waste with a coping saw, being careful to stay on the waste side of all the layout lines.

11. Pare to the baseline, working carefully in halfway from each side. Inspect the face of each pin and remove any material on the waste side of the layout line.

12. It's a good idea to test-fit the pieces before gluing them together. Tap the joint about halfway. If it seems too tight, take it apart and look for areas where the wood has been compressed or abraded. Pare carefully until the joint fits.

Half-Blind Dovetails

Half-blind dovetails, in which the joint is visible from only one face, are often a first choice for joining drawer faces to their sides. No end grain is visible from the front of the drawer. Marking and cutting the tails is essentially the same as for through dovetails (see pp. 14–15), with the exception that the tails are shorter to allow for a narrow section of end grain on the drawer front. As a rule of thumb, 3/16 in. is a good minimum thickness for this web.

With both parts of the joint cut, the pieces are nearly ready for assembly. But in the case of a drawer, grooves still need to be cut in the lower inside edge of the sides and front to accommodate the bottom. The back of the drawer is somewhat narrower; it comes down only as far as the drawer bottom. The drawer bottom is screwed to the back through a slot to allow for seasonal movement.

Grain orientation in the bottom of the drawer is important. It should run from side to side, not front to back. In summer, when the drawer bottom expands with higher humidity, the wood can grow to the back of the drawer. If the grain ran the other way, the drawer could be forced apart by the wood as it expanded.

Cutting half-blind dovetails

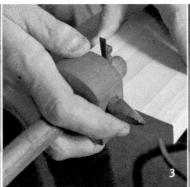

1. Scribe a line across the end of the drawer front with a cutting gauge. This line should be set back from the front of the drawer by about 3/16 in. Use this same cutting gauge to set the baseline for the tails at the front of the drawer side.

2. Align a drawer side to the scribed line and trace the outline of the tails onto the drawer front with a sharp pencil.

3. Scribe a line with a cutting gauge across the back of the drawer front that corresponds with the thickness of the drawer sides.

4. Fill out any portion of the line that wasn't transferred to the edge of the drawer front.

5. Next, use a square to continue the lines down the inside edge of the drawer front to the baseline.

6. After marking the areas to be cut away with a colored pencil to avoid any confusion, make the angled cuts that define the pins. Take care not to cut beyond either of the two scribed lines and stay on the waste side of the layout lines.

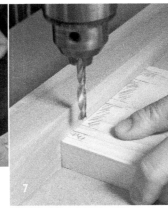

7. One way to remove the waste is with a drill press. Set the depth stop so the bit does not go beyond the layout line, and set the fence so the holes come nearly to the line on the inside of the drawer front.

8. After boring the first set of holes along the baseline, insert a shim to guide a parallel row of holes and remove more waste. The two rows of holes should nearly intersect.

9. Use a chisel to remove the waste up to the layout lines.

10. This drawer front (left) and drawer side (right) are nearly ready for assembly. But first, cut a groove in the two sides and the front to accommodate a drawer bottom. Position the groove so it will be hidden when the drawer is assembled.

11 & 12. Test-fit the pieces before final assembly. Fit the bottom, too. The grain is oriented from side to side, not front to back, so the drawer width won't be affected by seasonal dimensional changes in the drawer bottom.

13. The drawer bottom is held in place by one or two screws that go through a slot in the bottom into the drawer back. This allows the bottom of the drawer to move seasonally. Bevel the edges of the slot with a chisel so the screw head sits flush to the surface.

Making a Double-Lap Dovetail Joint

Double-lap dovetails are a mostly hidden joint that shows only a thin line of end grain on the edge of one face. What you can't see are the interlocking dovetails that give this joint its strength.

This joint can be cut so the end grain is visible either on the side or the front of the case. Here it's on the side so the joinery of the case matches the drawer. The tongue and pins are cut on the piece that will form the front of the case, then that piece is used to lay out the tails on the side piece.

Although laying out the joint may seem difficult at first, cutting the pins and tails is no different than it is for a conventional through or half-blind dovetail (see p. 14 and p. 16). Follow these steps and the photos and drawings on pp. 19–21.

Start by cutting a line off the inside face of the front that leaves the thickness of the tongue to the outside of the line *(photo and drawing 1 on the facing page)*. A safe minimum tongue width is 3/16 in.

Without changing the setting of the marking gauge, cut the baseline on the inside face of the side piece *(photo and drawing 2 on the facing page)*. Adjust a second cutting gauge to match the thickness of the side piece, then cut a baseline on the inside face of the front *(photo and drawing 3 on the facing page)*.

Set the height of a rabbeting bit in a router table so that it cuts to the line that defines the thickness of the tongue *(photo 4 on p. 20)*. The depth of cut determines the thickness of the web between the tails. Again, 3/16 in. is a safe minimum.

Because the joinery is hidden, strength becomes the primary concern in sizing the pins and tails. Making the pins and tails of equal size yields the most strength. A homemade dovetail gauge goes where no bevel gauge can reach *(photo 5 on p. 20)*.

Now cut out the pins. Marking the waste with a colored pencil helps minimize mistakes. A 1/8-in.-thick guard of oak keeps the sawblade from inadvertently damaging the inside of the tongue *(photo 6 on p. 20)*.

Set up a drill press to remove most of the waste between the saw cuts, then use a chisel to get the rest *(photo 7 on p. 20)*. Use a chisel to clean up all faces of the pins, paring carefully to the scribed lines *(photo 8 on p. 20)*. A really sharp chisel is a big help.

To define the thickness of the web between the tails, scribe a line off the end of the tongue to match the height of the tongue *(photo and drawing 9 on p. 21)*. Now you can mark out the tails on the inside face of the side by hooking the tongue over the end of the side and using the pins as your guide *(photo 10 on p. 21)*. Make sure the pencil is very sharp so it makes a thin line.

Now it's back to the drill press to drill out most of the waste, then use a chisel to pare to the lines and define the tails *(photo 11 on p. 21)*.

Test the joint without glue *(photo 12 on p. 21)*. Front and side pieces are labeled in blue pencil. If you have to make any adjustments in how the joint fits, now is the time to do it.

Double-Lap Dovetails

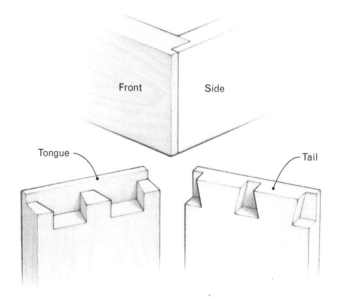

Front   Side

Tongue   Tail

Cutting double-lap dovetails

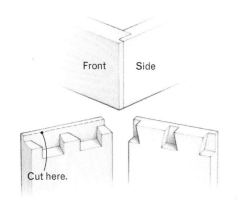
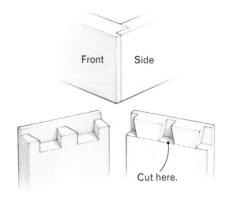
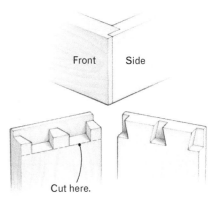

1. Use a marking gauge to cut a line off the inside face of the front.

2. With the same setting, cut the baseline on the inside face of the side piece.

3. With a second cutting gauge cut a baseline on the inside face of the front.

4. Use a rabbeting bit in a router table to cut to the line defining the thickness of the tongue.

5. A homemade dovetail gauge is useful for laying out the pins.

6. When cutting out the pins, be careful not to damage the inside of the tongue.

7. Remove most of the waste between the sawcuts on a drill press, and finish with a chisel.

8. Clean up carefully with a sharp chisel.

9. Scribe a line off the end of the tongue.

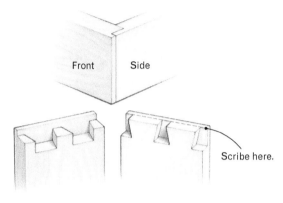

Front   Side

Scribe here.

10. Use the pins as a guide for laying out the tails on the inside face of the side piece.

11. Hog out the waste on the drill press and pare with a chisel.

12. Test-fit the joint before gluing up.

Mitered Corners

Carcase miters are appropriate where clean lines are a high priority. The face grain of the chest front wraps around the mitered corners without the interruption of stiles (as in a frame-and-panel carcase) or visible joinery (as is the case with dovetails). In veneered work, this same lack of visible joinery serves to keep any core materials hidden from view.

Tablesaw, router table, or shaper can all produce the accuracy and consistency necessary to make clean and true miters. Testing cuts in scrap that matches your finished material is the only way to check for square and that the angle of the cut is dead accurate. The surface of this cut is a combination of long grain and end grain, not optimal for strong glue joints. Splines, keys, biscuits, and Dominos are all good means for reinforcing miters to provide strength and durability.

Tablesaw Jig for Cutting Miters

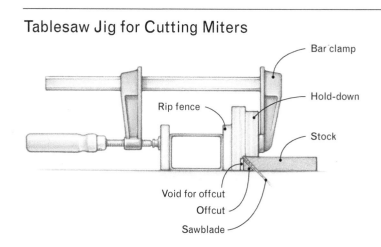

Bar clamp
Hold-down
Rip fence
Stock
Void for offcut
Offcut
Sawblade

Cutting and assembling miters

1. In preparation for the cuts, the blade of the tablesaw is tilted to 45 degrees. Into a length of scrap, cut a ¼-in.-deep rabbet, making it 1/16 in. narrower than the thickness of the workpiece, and clamp it to the tablesaw fence. Now add a hold-down with another set of clamps. These steps will help to prevent the offcut from binding between the fence and the blade.

2. The most accurate test is to cut bevels on the ends of four equal pieces of scrap and tape them together at the corners to form a box. Any errors will be obvious. In this case, the blade is set at an angle slightly less than 45 degrees and should be adjusted.

3. Check the ends of each workpiece with a square.

4. Make the cuts. Because the rabbet in the auxiliary fence isn't quite as high as the workpiece is thick, there's a small shoulder for the workpiece to ride against. The gap gives a place for the offcut to go—but don't stand in the kickback zone. The technique is not foolproof.

5. After marking out biscuit locations on the end of the workpiece, make the cuts with a biscuit joiner. A small block clamped to the fence helps to stabilize the tool. It's a good idea to make a test cut first on scrap.

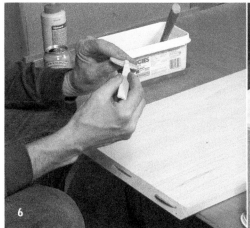

6. To minimize problems during final assembly, glue the biscuits into one side of each joint first.

7. Special cauls made for the occasion are worth the effort and the expense. Triangular pieces of material glued and screwed to the edges of ¼-in. plywood will make it easy to clamp corners tightly together. The plywood pieces should be slightly shorter than the corresponding sides of the box.

8. Now it's time to test-fit. A band clamp may be useful for holding the cauls in place while clamping pressure is applied. Work your way around the box with clamps, check the fit, and make any adjustments before gluing up the pieces.

Details

Hinges and locksets are common finishing details for a chest. Although some makers produce wood or metal hinges of their own design (see Ted Blachly's chest on p. 96), there are many high-quality metal hinges on the market in iron, brass, nickel, and other finishes. The most common varieties include butt hinges, which come with either fixed or removable pins and are installed as pairs into mortises; strap hinges, which distribute the weight of the lid, and the strain of opening and closing it, over a greater area; piano hinges, which span the full length of the opening and provide a hardy connection thanks to screws every inch or two; and torsion hinges, which are surface-mounted to allow the lid to hold any open position.

Installing a pair of butt hinges is straightforward, and can be accomplished entirely by hand or with the help of a router, as shown below.

Adding a mortised lockset and escutcheon to a chest keeps its contents more secure and also adds a classy level of fit and finish. Many types of locks are available and the details of installation may vary somewhat from type to type. The photos on the facing page show how to install a half-mortise lock in a drawer front.

Installing a mortise hinge

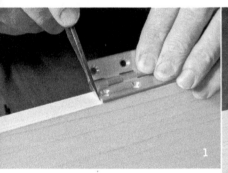

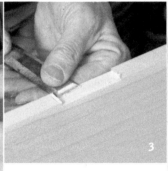
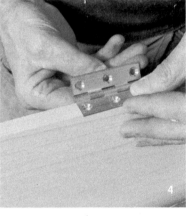

1. Mark the ends of the hinge mortise directly from the hinge.

2. Using a laminate trimmer or small router, remove the waste inside the layout lines. Set the depth of the cut off the back of the hinge to the center of the pin, and test the setup on scrap before cutting the mortise in the workpiece.

3. Now use a chisel to cut all the way to the layout lines.

4. The hinge should fit snugly in the mortise. The edge of the workpiece and the top of the hinge leaf should be flush.

Installing a half-mortise lock

1. The first step is to lay out the width of the mortise for the lock on the top edge of the drawer front. A piece of scrap clamped to the drawer front will position the lock correctly front to back.

2. Use a router or laminate trimmer to remove the waste inside the layout lines. The depth of the cut should equal the thickness of the lock casing.

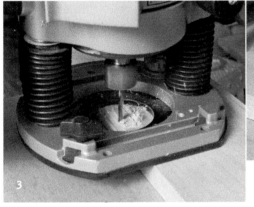

3. Now lay out the outline of the lock body on the inside face of the drawer and use a router to remove the waste. The depth of the cut should equal the thickness of the lock body (the fattest part of the lock assembly).

4. Clean up the mortise with a chisel. Then place the lock in the mortise and mark the outlines of the lock casing on the back of the drawer. Use a router or laminate trimmer to remove this waste.

5. When fitted correctly, the lock is flush with the top of the drawer and the back of the drawer. To complete the installation, drill a hole through the drawer front for the key and install an escutcheon.

Wood Movement

No matter how exacting a furniture maker is with the joinery, a piece can be ruined by seasonal wood movement. A board moves in all three dimensions, but the changes tangentially (across the face of a flatsawn board) are the most dramatic and must be accounted for in the design and construction of any case piece. Trap a piece of solid lumber and either it will crack or buckle or its enclosure will crack.

The process of calculating the annual movement of a specific species requires a bit of measuring and some basic math. Start by measuring the width of the board; the wider the board, the greater the range of movement. Next, calculate the annual change in moisture content. Thankfully, the Forest Products Laboratory (FPL) has done the research to give us typical minimum and maximum moisture content readings by location across the United States (see the maps on the facing page). The result of subtracting the smaller value (January) from the larger value (July) yields the annual change in moisture content.

The last value for this equation is the movement coefficient, which adjusts for the differing behaviors of individual species and how each was sawn. Again, the FPL has compiled a table that offers two values for each species—one for flatsawn material and one for quartersawn. Multiplying these three figures yields the approximate measurement of the annual change in width due to changing moisture content. By noting the time of year, one can determine whether a board is expanding or contracting and where it sits in the cycle.

Allowing for Wood Movement

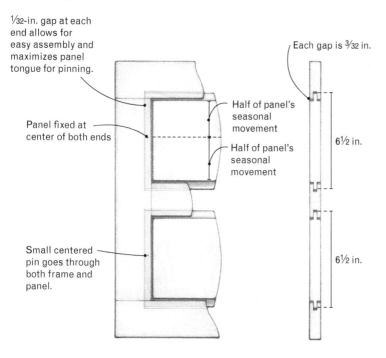

1/32-in. gap at each end allows for easy assembly and maximizes panel tongue for pinning.

Panel fixed at center of both ends

Half of panel's seasonal movement

Half of panel's seasonal movement

Small centered pin goes through both frame and panel.

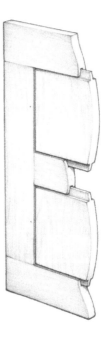

Each gap is 3/32 in.

6½ in.

6½ in.

Seasonal Moisture Content

In most of the United States, the average moisture content of interior woodwork varies from winter to summer. It's those seasonal changes that cause wood to shrink in winter and expand in summer.

**MOISTURE CONTENT OF
INTERIOR WOODWORK IN JANUARY**

**MOISTURE CONTENT OF
INTERIOR WOODWORK IN JULY**

Movement Value of Wood		
SPECIES	QUARTERSAWN	FLATSAWN
Alder (Red)	0.0015	0.0026
Ash (White)	0.0017	0.0027
Aspen (Quaking)	0.0012	0.0023
Basswood (American)	0.0023	0.0033
Beech (American)	0.0019	0.0043
Birch (Yellow)	0.0026	0.0034
Butternut	0.0012	0.0022
Cherry (Black)	0.0013	0.0025
Fir (Balsam)	0.0001	0.0024
Mahogany	0.0017	0.0024
Maple (Red)	0.0014	0.0029
Maple (Sugar)	0.0017	0.0035
Oak (Red)	0.0016	0.0037
Oak (White)	0.0018	0.0037
Pine (Eastern White)	0.0007	0.0021
Pine (Longleaf)	0.0018	0.0037
Pine (Ponderosa)	0.0013	0.0022
Pine (Sugar)	0.0010	0.0019
Poplar (Yellow)	0.0016	0.0029
Sweetgum	0.0018	0.0037
Sycamore (American)	0.0017	0.0030
Teak	0.0010	0.0019
Walnut (Black)	0.0019	0.0027

**MOISTURE
CONTENT (%)**

- <4%
- 4–5
- 5–6
- 6–7
- 7–8
- 8–9
- 9–10
- 10–11
- 11–12
- 12–13
- 13–14

Waterfall Chest

Taking a clue from nature

BRIAN SARGENT
Candia, New Hampshire

DIMENSIONS
22¼ in. deep, 56 in. wide,
24½ in. high

MATERIALS
Lacewood and Swiss pear
veneers, Italian poplar
bending plywood, solid Swiss
pear, stainless steel

HARDWARE
Stainless-steel butt hinges,
leather strap lid stay

FINISH
Shellac and wax

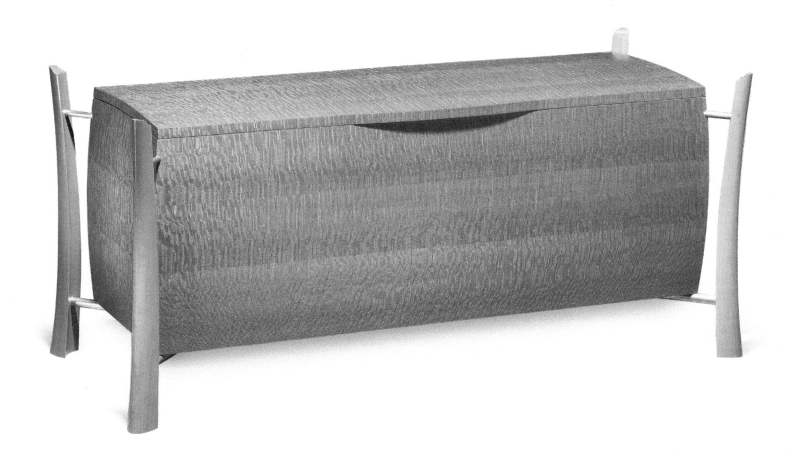

New Hampshire furniture master Brian Sargent is no great fan of the straight line. Suspended in air by four stainless-steel posts, this lacewood chest is a case in point. The chest gets its name from the pattern of its lacewood veneer. Sargent laid it up so the surface would look like water cascading from a waterfall and splashing as it came to Earth.

Sargent designed the chest for the end of a king-size bed. It's a horizontal version of a lingerie cabinet he had made earlier for the same room. "The client is a woman, so the design of the chest has a more feminine feel," Sargent says. "The softness of the pearwood legs and interior of the chest reflect the character of the client, and the fluidity of the lacewood creates a calming expression."

The opposing curves of the legs and chest sides help the piece seem sturdy and well grounded, as if four tusks had been planted in the ground to hold the chest firmly in place. The gentle curves of the sides and lid seem effortless, but in truth, they're not. Sargent started by making a mold that would be used to form the sides, front and back, and lid of the case. When the mold was complete, he laid up layers of 1/8-in. Italian bending plywood and veneer—lacewood on the outside, pear on the inside—and put the sandwich into a vacuum press (see the sidebar on p. 31). The sides of the case are 1 in. thick: nine plies of bending plywood plus the veneer.

Sargent veneered just the inside surfaces of the side pieces, then cut the miters for all four corners on a tablesaw sled. The sides of the case were veneered after the case was glued together, its corners reinforced with biscuits. Sargent used a slow-set glue, Unibond 800, for a long open time. The Swiss pear interior was prefinished and hand-rubbed before the chest was assembled.

If that procedure seems complicated, Sargent still had to drill holes for the upper stainless-steel support pins directly into the mitered corners of the case. He did that by making two matched sets of legs, one in pear and the other in poplar. All eight legs were drilled for the pins in the same way, except that holes in the top of the poplar legs went all the way through. When the chest and its frame were assembled temporarily with the poplar legs, the holes provided an accurate guide for drilling into the corners of the case. Sargent applied tape to the case where the holes would be bored, used a very sharp brad-point bit, and hoped for the best. Tearout was virtually nonexistent.

The stainless pins at the bottom are linked to two Y-shaped connectors, which in turn are welded to a straight section of rod. No drilling there. ▪

OPPOSITE Although it's not apparent from a distance, all of the exterior faces of this chest, except for the bottom, are curved. To make the pieces, Brian Sargent laid up layers of veneer and bending plywood on a mold that could be placed inside a vacuum press.

ABOVE Swiss pear on the inside, lacewood on the outside. Sargent calls the piece the "Waterfall Chest" after the cascading figure of the lacewood.

Waterfall Chest

Brian Sargent's lacewood veneer case is captured between its tusk-like legs by stainless-steel rods. Connections at the upper corners are made by boring holes directly into the corners of the case. At the bottom, rods support the case from below without actually piercing it. All of the cabinet faces are curved.

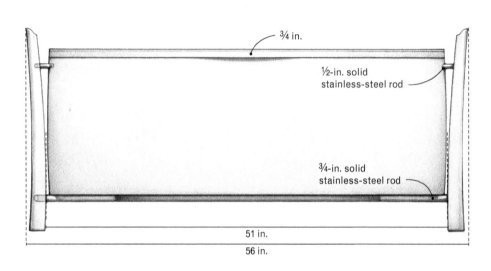

¾ in.

½-in. solid stainless-steel rod

¾-in. solid stainless-steel rod

51 in.

56 in.

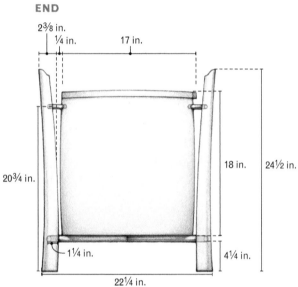

2⅜ in.

¼ in.

17 in.

20¾ in.

18 in.

24½ in.

1¼ in.

4¼ in.

22¼ in.

MAKING CURVED CHEST PARTS

Brian Sargent's chest is made from subtly curved panels of lacewood and Swiss pear veneers over a core of Italian poplar plywood. To form the curved parts, Sargent started by building a mold from ¾-in. plywood, two layers of ⅜-in. bending plywood, a single layer of Italian poplar plywood, and a skin of plastic laminate. Solid wood ribs cut to the right curve and attached to the plywood base give the parts their graceful shape. The ⅜-in. bending ply conforms to this shape, and the Italian poplar creates an extremely smooth and precise foundation for the veneer.

Once the mold was ready, Sargent laid up the pieces for a chest part: Swiss pear veneer for the interior, nine layers of ⅛-in. Italian poplar, lacewood veneer for the outside of the case, and a sheet of plastic laminate to prevent the glue in the assembly from sticking to anything. Then it was off to the vacuum press for an overnight clamping.

When the part was cured, Sargent still had to cut it to its finish size, as well as cut the miters on the case sides. He made a sled from medium-density fiberboard, with contoured ribs that fit the curve of the chest piece, placed the piece to be cut on top, and ran them both through the tablesaw.

1. Each chest component is a sandwich of Italian poplar plywood and veneer, clamped to a curved mold in a vacuum press.

2. Parts were trimmed to size and mitered on a tablesaw. A sled made from medium density fiberboard carried the sides of the chest for the miter cut.

Veneer and plywood sandwich

Chest components consist of multiple layers of Italian poplar plywood and veneer. The mold to which this sandwich is clamped in a vacuum press is no less complex.

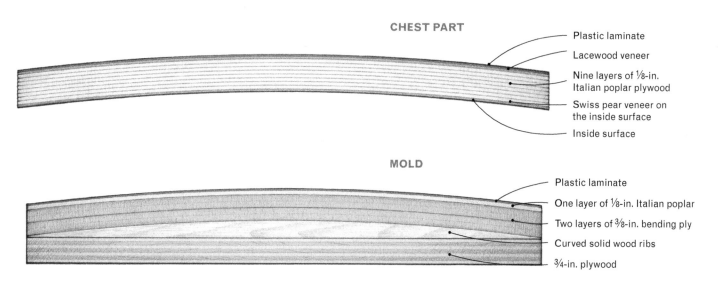

CHEST PART

- Plastic laminate
- Lacewood veneer
- Nine layers of ⅛-in. Italian poplar plywood
- Swiss pear veneer on the inside surface
- Inside surface

MOLD

- Plastic laminate
- One layer of ⅛-in. Italian poplar
- Two layers of ⅜-in. bending ply
- Curved solid wood ribs
- ¾-in. plywood

Bermudan Chest

Saving period details from obscurity

AUSTIN MATHESON
Rockport, Maine

DIMENSIONS
22 in. deep, 51 in. wide,
30 in. high

MATERIALS
Mahogany, Spanish cedar
bottom, maple and holly inlay

HARDWARE
Brass harpsichord hinges

FINISH
Oil/varnish

eave the Newport block-front secretaries to someone else. The interests of Maine furniture maker Austin Kane Matheson lie with more obscure styles of furniture like this Bermudan chest on frame. As Matheson, a 2003 graduate of the North Bennet Street School in Boston, explains it, the style developed in the 17th century as Bermudan craftsmen devised portable storage that met their unique needs.

"The Bermudan chest on frame is a style of furniture unique to Bermuda," he says. "It is said that its popularity stems from the fact that it was easily transported onboard a ship and was effective at keeping unwanted insects out. The Bermudan people have always been a seafaring culture in a semitropical environment, so these two benefits would make sense."

The style remained popular until the 19th century, a very long run. Some details changed with the times. Legs might variously be bun feet, as is the case here, or either cabriole or Chippendale, depending on what style was current at the time.

Matheson didn't copy any particular chest in creating this one, but used design elements from two pieces. Although the overall proportions are typical for the period, the bun feet are copies from a chest from the 17th century, whereas the scrollwork on the bottom of the frame comes from the 18th century. He looked at many examples of the style in a rare-book library before choosing the design details he found appealing. The inlaid maple and holly shell on the lid, on the other hand, is of his own design.

Chests like this would have been made of Bermudan cedar, Matheson says, one of only a dozen and a half land-growing plants endemic to the islands that is now virtually extinct. The trees grew to 50 ft. in height and 24 in. across at the butt. When the cedar became harder to find, craftsmen started using mahogany, which was Matheson's choice here.

Construction is traditional: a dovetailed case, mortise-and-tenon base, and a lid with breadboard ends. The chest is not screwed or otherwise fastened to the frame, but rests on top of the frame inside the molding. Dovetails here are conventional, although Matheson might be tempted to try the more decorative Bermudan dovetails if he were to make the case again.

(CONTINUED)

OPPOSITE Austin Matheson's chest on frame is an adaptation of 17th- and 18th-century furniture made in the islands of Bermuda. This one has bun feet, but others of the era might have had different leg styles.

ABOVE An inlaid shell on the top of the chest is made from holly and maple, a detail of Matheson's own design.

The scrollwork along the bottom of the chest is a detail borrowed from an 18th-century Bermudan chest.

Inside the chest is a till, a small compartment to one side with its own lid. Pieces of the till, including the top, are let into the sides of the case and all of it is glued up at one time. There were no second chances for the lid, because it could not be trimmed once the case was in place. It had to fit correctly the first time. The till does hold one surprise, a small drawer hidden behind its front face. The drawer is accessible only when the face is pushed upward in a ⅝-in.-deep groove cut in the side of the case.

"I'm always interested in the more obscure styles of furniture that reflect a unique evolution in relative isolation," Matheson says. "The needs of the Bermudan people differed from those in America and Europe at the time and so the furniture evolved in a slightly different manner. From a design perspective, I love the bun feet and the lively scroll work of the apron." ▪

Parts of the interior till are trapped in grooves cut into the sides of the case, meaning that all of it was glued together at once. The fit of the lid had to be correct.

Bermudan Chest

The dovetailed mahogany case sits inside a band of molding on the base but is not attached with screws or other fasteners. The lid has breadboard ends.

PLAN VIEW

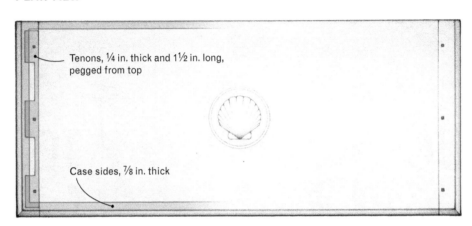

Tenons, ¼ in. thick and 1½ in. long, pegged from top

Case sides, ⅞ in. thick

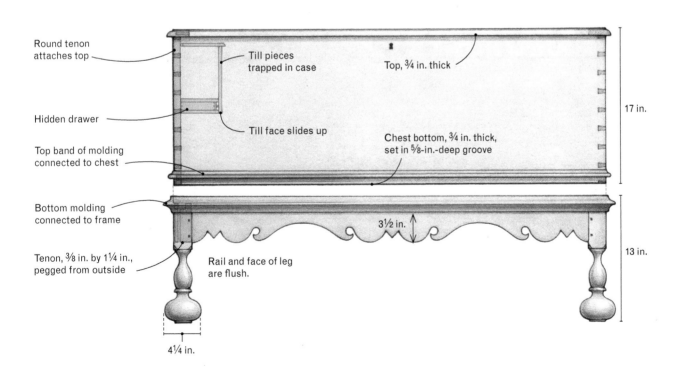

Round tenon attaches top

Till pieces trapped in case

Top, ¾ in. thick

Hidden drawer

Till face slides up

Chest bottom, ¾ in. thick, set in ⅝-in.-deep groove

Top band of molding connected to chest

17 in.

Bottom molding connected to frame

3½ in.

Tenon, ⅜ in. by 1¼ in., pegged from outside

Rail and face of leg are flush.

13 in.

4¼ in.

Red Leaf Chest

Moving color and texture to the forefront

MICHAEL CULLEN
Petaluma, California

DIMENSIONS
15⅛ in. deep, 32 in. wide,
23 in. high

MATERIALS
Mahogany, wenge (lid frame
and base), Port Orford cedar
(bottom)

FINISH
Milk paint with thin coat of
shellac; base and interior,
shellac; bottom unfinished

A wide plank of curly cherry or spalted maple can quickly turn a blanket chest into a treatise on the natural wonders of wood. There are a number of examples of that elsewhere in this book, but Michael Cullen is traveling in another direction.

The mahogany carcase and lid of this blanket chest are a canvas where Cullen has used carving tools and paint to create a swirling pattern of leaves. What natural wood does show—the wenge in the base and lid frame—is subdued and complementary.

Cullen has experimented with a variety of styles during his 20-plus-year career. He first approached surface design with jigs and routers but found the results were listless. Cullen turned instead to carving tools and looked to nature for inspiration. He realized that in nature no patterns were perfect and by letting his approach become looser the results were far more satisfying.

He designed the leaf motif for this chest on paper and followed with a carved and painted sample. After the chest was built, Cullen sketched the design directly on the surface of the chest, but "without making much of a fuss," and started to carve. It's not a paint-by-numbers approach. Choices presented themselves and he found himself altering his original patterns slightly as the work progressed. In his work, it's not a lack of precision but a matter of leaving room for refinement. When he finished, the leaves were flowing from one surface to the next as if they were falling from trees or being swept along by the wind.

Color is the last important element in his work, and here, too, Cullen left himself some slack. He started with a plan as he worked the milk paint into the surface, and continued playing with it until he got the colors he wanted. "Unlike woodworking," he says, "you can apply and subtract paint until the desired effect is achieved. I never have a strong or, shall I say, locked-in sense of what it should be. And I like it that way because it leaves a lot of room for discovery."

The sides of the chest are joined with splined miters, a joint that Cullen likes because it doesn't create any visual distractions. The lid is a $\frac{1}{2}$-in.-thick panel set into the frame with a $\frac{1}{8}$-in. reveal at the perimeter. The frame is mitered with floating tenons made of wenge. The bottom of the box is unfinished Port Orford cedar.

Joinery for the miters on the lid frame are floating tenons made of wenge, $1\frac{3}{4}$ in. by $\frac{3}{8}$ in., that are placed so they don't interfere with the panels. The mitered box of the chest is splined together with $\frac{1}{8}$-in. bending poplar. Grooves for the splines are stopped so the spline is invisible and held away from the bottom so they don't interfere with the panel there. The chest body is stepped in $\frac{1}{8}$ in. all the way around and held to the stand with two screws.

(CONTINUED)

"I have made this chest many times," he says, "and each time I do it a little differently. I still find myself fascinated by the proportions of such a simple form. Each time, I adjust the height-to-length-to-depth proportions, and yet there always seems to be room for more discovery and refinement. One thing that I am particularly interested in is straying far from conventional proportions of most chest designs. I like my chests to stand high and appear a bit narrow in their depth."

The base and frame for the top also are opportunities for a little experimentation. Cullen says at some point in the process he stops and takes time to make samples of some pieces, changing the width of the frame on top, for example, or altering the shape of the feet. "There are a lot of subtle changes with these particular parts that change what the final piece will look like," he says. "My main objective is to make the chest appear light on its feet yet stable."

Red Leaf Chest

Michael Cullen's Red Leaf Chest is made from mahogany and joined at the corners with splined miters. There is no exposed joinery or seams to interfere with the pattern of carved leaves.

FRONT

SIDE

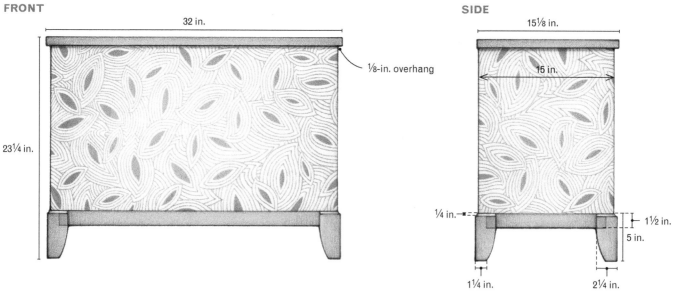

32 in.

⅛-in. overhang

23¼ in.

15⅛ in.

15 in.

¼ in.

1½ in.

5 in.

1¼ in.

2¼ in.

TOP

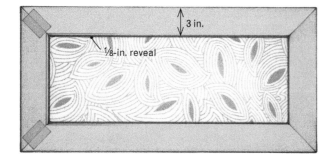

3 in.

⅛-in. reveal

A CARVER'S REPERTOIRE

The carved and painted faces of these chests are a signature detail of the work of Michael Cullen. He sketches the patterns by hand after a piece has been assembled, "without making much of a fuss," and leaves room for adjustments as he carves. Multiple coats of milk paint and shellac complete the finish.

ABOVE *Blue Chest* (2000) is made of mahogany with a wenge frame and stand. The lining is Port Orford cedar.
Dimensions: 15⅛ in. deep, 32 in. wide, 23¼ in. high.

ABOVE RIGHT *Chest on Stand* (2009) is carved and painted mahogany with a Spanish cedar interior.
Dimensions: 14 in. deep, 25 in. wide, 32 in. high.

RIGHT *A Chest for a New Idea* (2010) is made from walnut taken from the Mount Vernon estate of George Washington and finished with milk paint and shellac. The interior is unfinished.
Dimensions: 11 in. deep, 27 in. wide, 30 in. high.

CARVED LEAVES

Michael Cullen's work is frequently enriched with carved surfaces, as is his mahogany blanket chest aptly named the Red Leaf Chest. Case sides are joined with spline miter joints; there are no intersecting lines or joinery that would be visible with a dovetailed or frame-and-panel chest. That leaves the field free of interference for a carved pattern that wraps seamlessly around the sides.

Cullen makes the chest first, then carves the surface. Here he demonstrates the multistep process on a piece of mahogany. He starts by laying out the design on the faces of the chest freehand with a pencil *(photo 1)*. The leaves are carved into the surface with a tool called a veiner and a mallet *(photo 2)*.

At the center of each leaf is a textured area made with a small gouge *(photo 3)*. Cullen works inward toward an incised line from opposite sides of the leaf.

Although Cullen has a good idea of what he wants the carved surface to look like, he leaves room for adjustments as he goes. The result is a pleasingly organic flavor to the pattern of overlapping leaves *(photo 4)*.

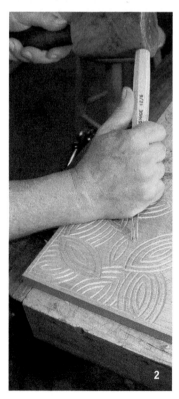

1. After the case is built, Cullen sketches the leaves with a pencil.

2. Cullen carves the surface with a veiner and mallet.

3. A gouge adds detail at the center of each leaf.

4. Carving complete, the surface now gets a finish.

With the carving finished, Cullen applies layers of milk paint to the surface. In this case, he starts with an undercoat of black followed by two topcoats of red *(photo 5)*. Sanding the surface with 320-grit paper allows some of the black undercoat to pop out while simultaneously smoothing the surface *(photo 6)*. Cullen gives the surface a final buffing with 4/0 steel wool.

To protect and seal the surface, Cullen finishes the chest with shellac. It also helps to deepen the color of the milk paint *(photo 7)*. The finished panel has a rich, multi-dimensional look *(photo 8)*.

5. The mahogany gets a black milk paint undercoat and two red topcoats.

6. Some of the black pops out when the surface is sanded with 320-grit paper.

7. Shellac seals the surface and deepens the color.

8. The completed panel.

Plain and Simple

Graceful style and an economy of detail

JOHN McALEVEY
Warren, Maine

DIMENSIONS	MATERIALS	HARDWARE	FINISH
18½ in. deep, 43 in. wide, 20 in. high	Walnut	Butt hinges, leather strap for lid	Watco® mixed with varnish

John McAlevey got interested in making furniture after seeing an exhibit of contemporary work and visiting woodworking shops that especially interested him. That was in 1962, and he's been at it ever since. In the intervening years, McAlevey's work has come to reflect a method that, in his words, "emphasizes an economy of design, making, and use of materials." He works exclusively in solid wood, and his outlook, like his furniture, is straightforward and without pretense.

He likes primitive New England furniture and thinks Scandinavian designs also have had an impact. "I can't say my style has changed too much over the years," he says. "I consider myself to be a remnant of the designer-craftsman movement that took place after World War II and continued up until the craftspeople became obsessed with being thought of as artists."

This walnut chest is put together with simple joinery. On the front and back, the top and bottom rails are mortised into the curved pieces that serve as both the panel stiles and the chest's legs. The solid ends of the chest are attached to the inside of the legs with biscuits. The bottom, also a solid panel, is attached with biscuits to the ends of the chest and also glued and screwed from the bottom to the lower edge of the stretchers. The edge of the panel protrudes slightly beyond the edge of the stretcher and creates a slight reveal.

The top has breadboard ends, and other than the wood itself, there is no other ornamentation. The lid is kept in place with a leather strap. "It's a well-designed piece of furniture," McAlevey says, "and it does its job."

McAlevey developed the design with some sketches and a scale drawing. With all of his designs, he works out some of the details, including the joinery, as he goes and avoids making prototypes unless he's working on a new chair design.

In addition to making chairs, tables, and case pieces, McAlevey also is a bowl turner. He turns the wood on the lathe while it's still green and then begins applying a finish. As the green wood dries, the shape of the bowl changes a little bit and gives it a slightly out-of-round shape. On the bottom of each he signs his name and draws a picture of a dog, a tradition he's beginning to extend to the furniture he makes. ▪

OPPOSITE John McAlevey's walnut blanket chest shows a restrained stylistic hand and an appreciation for both Scandinavian and primitive American designs.

ABOVE A leather strap keeps the lid from opening too far. It's held by brass screws and grommets.

Plain and Simple

John McAlevely drew on more than four decades of experience in designing and building this chest.
It shows an economy of materials and straightforward construction. The legs double as panel stiles for
the front and back of the case. The ends are glued to the legs, with biscuits ensuring alignment with the
inside of the leg.

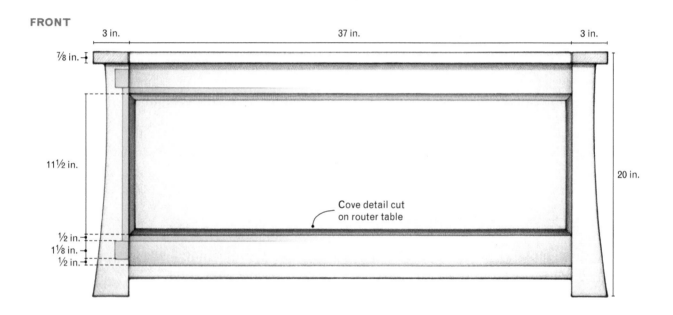

FRONT

3 in.

37 in.

3 in.

⅞ in.

11½ in.

20 in.

Cove detail cut
on router table

½ in.

1⅛ in.

½ in.

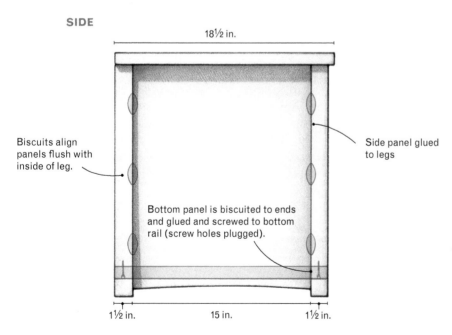

SIDE

18½ in.

Biscuits align
panels flush with
inside of leg.

Side panel glued
to legs

Bottom panel is biscuited to ends
and glued and screwed to bottom
rail (screw holes plugged).

1½ in.

15 in.

1½ in.

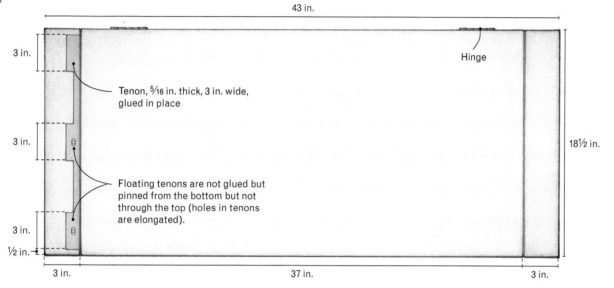

43 in.

3 in.

Hinge

Tenon, 5⁄16 in. thick, 3 in. wide, glued in place

3 in.

18½ in.

Floating tenons are not glued but pinned from the bottom but not through the top (holes in tenons are elongated).

3 in.

½ in.

3 in.

37 in.

3 in.

CHEST FOR AN AUCTION

This walnut blanket chest was originally made for the 2003 auction of the New Hampshire Furniture Master's Association (www.furnituremasters.org), a unique annual event that benefits both New England artisans and collectors of handmade furniture. A number of other furniture masters are represented in this book, including Ted Blachly, Jeffrey Cooper, Garrett Hack, Terry Moore, Brian Reid, and Brian Sargent. The organization has helped furniture makers sell their work while broadening both the public's understanding of the process and an appreciation for craftsmanship.

PINNING PANELS

In frame-and-panel construction, panels are sized so they can shrink and expand across the grain seasonally without affecting the frame itself. Solid wood panels should not be glued in, but pinning the center of the panel at each end keeps an even reveal at the perimeter and allows the panel to move with changes in humidity.

Start by adjusting the panel in the frame so the reveal (the space between the edge of the panel and the frame) is consistent. Pry the panel gently with a putty knife or thin piece of wood to move it into position (*photo 1*). Spacers can help keep the reveal even.

Strike a line at the center of the frame. Lay out the pin location so it is halfway across the portion of the panel that's in the groove of the frame. In this case, the groove is 1/2 in. deep and the panel extends into it by 7/16 in., so the pin will be set about 7/32 in. from the edge of the frame (*photo 2*).

Drill a pilot hole that's slightly smaller than the diameter of the pin (*photo 3*). This pin, a 4d brad, will go all the way through, but

1. Adjust the panel so the reveal is even.

2. Lay out locations for the pins.

3. Drill a pilot hole for the pin.

pins also can be inserted from the back side and stopped before they reach the face. Pins can be metal or wood.

Drive the nail through the frame *(photo 4)*, clip off the excess with a pair of diagonal cutters *(photo 5)* (watch your eyes), and file the stub flat *(photo 6)*.

A simpler alternative is to pin the panel back by shooting a small air nail or pin from the back.

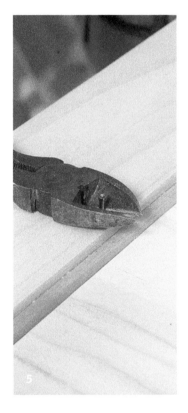

4. Drive the pin through the frame and panel.

5. Clip off the excess.

6. File the end flat. If the pin is wood, cut off the excess with a chisel.

A Chest for Life

Storage designed to suit many needs

LAURA MAYS
Salruck, Renvyle, County Galway, Ireland

DIMENSIONS	MATERIALS	HARDWARE	FINISH
19⅝ in. deep, 31½ in. wide, 15¾ in. high	Irish sycamore	Steel butt hinges, fabric-tape lid stays	Shellac

aura Mays's idea was to build a single chest that was not too specific in function so it could be used by someone through many stages of life: as a toy chest, for clothes storage, or for linens, depending on the need. Plus, the top would be at a good height for sitting.

One of this chest's most notable features is a concave, slatted lid, just the opposite of what we're used to seeing on traditional steamer trunks in which vacationers once carried their belongings (tops were curved as insurance against damage: they couldn't be stacked). Mays built this one with an inward arc because it would be less likely to become a catchall for household objects. The curve at the bottom of the case is there to complement the top but also to make it easier to pick up the chest.

The chest is made from Irish sycamore, not quite the same thing botanically as the great mottled trees called sycamore in the United States. In Ireland, Mays says, sycamore (*Acer pseudoplatunus*) grows almost like a weed, and it's not often used for lumber because it doesn't get big enough. Mays could get the wood only in narrow planks, and she used the width as a module for planning the chest—the carcase is three planks high, and the lid is one plank high. She wasn't thrilled with the selection, but in the end she liked the wood and its inherent flaws.

Although construction of the case seemed straightforward, the lid with its slats was something of a puzzle whose exact details Mays worked out as she went. She was reluctant to make the carcase and lid as one unit and cut them apart later because the glue-up just seemed too daunting. Instead, she made the two parts separately, taking great pains to make the top precisely enough that it would fit the case perfectly.

Were she to build the chest again, Mays says she'd make the lid lighter by reducing its height and reducing the number of intermediate supports from two to one.

Mays began studying furniture making at the Galway Mayo Institute of Technology in 1995, where she now teaches furniture design and manufacture full time. But it was the two years she spent at the College of the Redwoods in Fort Bragg, California, that seems to have had the most lasting impact on her sense of design.

(CONTINUED)

OPPOSITE Laura Mays based the design of this chest at least in part on the width of the sycamore planks she could get. The carcase is three planks high, the lid one plank high.

ABOVE Mays used fabric tape for the lid stays, one on each side.

There is often a similarity of style among graduates of this woodworking program, no surprise given the powerful influence of James Krenov. But not so much for Mays, who says it was Krenov's approach, his "sincerity, honesty, and questioning," that were at the heart of her education there. As with most furniture makers, Mays finds her style has changed over time. "I've become increasingly interested in details," she says, "realizing that details can alter the whole experience and meaning of a piece. Also, I've become more aware that experiencing a piece of furniture involves all the senses, not just sight, and that the meaning and value of a piece changes over time as the piece reveals itself to us." ▪

With no specialized compartments or interior details, the chest could serve many potential uses. Mays hoped it would follow its owner through life, adapting to whatever need presented itself.

A Chest for Life

The slats in the curved top of this chest are connected by full length, loose splines, and their ends let into a groove in the ends of the lid. The bottom of the chest is a solid panel let into grooves in the sides and left to float. It's supported by two rails below, similar to those under the top of the lid.

TOP

SIDE

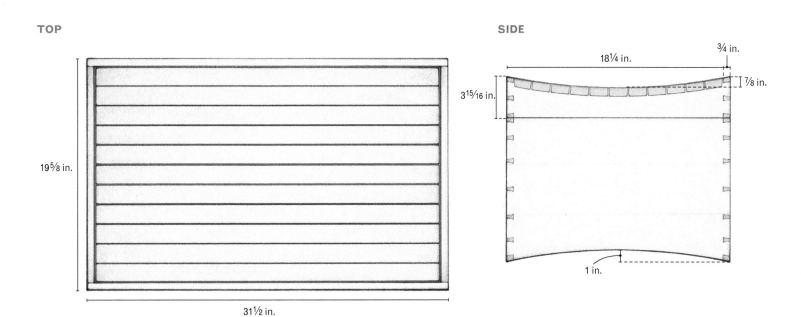

FRONT

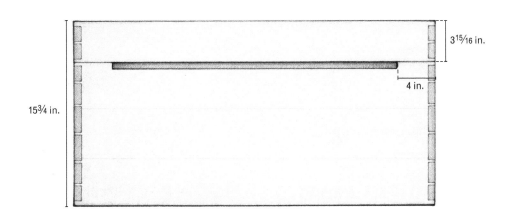

Modern Lines

Practical storage and a contemporary feel

LIBBY SCHRUM
Camden, Maine

DIMENSIONS	MATERIALS	HARDWARE	FINISH
18 in. deep, 48 in. wide, 18 in. high	Maple, quartersawn maple veneer	Torsion hinge lid support, metal ferrules, drawer slides	Shellac

After taking a three-month course at the Center for Furniture Craftsmanship in 2001, Libby Schrum went on to earn a master's degree from the Rhode Island School of Design, returned to Maine, and eventually began building high-end yacht interiors as well as furniture on commission.

Her initial interest in Arts and Crafts, Shaker, and Asian design gradually gave way to more modern work, as evidenced by the crisp lines and unadorned exterior of this contemporary chest in maple and maple veneer.

Schrum wanted the blanket chest to use space more efficiently than a simple box with a lid. Bulky items can go in the main storage compartment, but there also are two drawers—on low-profile metal slides—where other things may be tucked away without getting lost.

Schrum liked the idea of the slab ends on the chest (they measure 1¼ in. thick), but she didn't want to expose a lot of edge grain at the top. So she made chest components from plywood banded with solid material and then veneered both sides. Beneath the upholstery, the lid is of frame-and-panel construction, as are the bottom of the chest and the intermediate divider between the chest itself and the drawers.

"I found it quite challenging to get all the miters on the corners of the edge-banding perfect," she says. "Perfect miters will give the piece that seamless look, but flushing up the edge-banding can be tricky." Just about any technique had its hazards, Schrum discovered, and the complex drawer fronts with their rectangular cutouts were especially time-consuming.

Drawer boxes are made from ½-in.-thick soft maple, joined at the corners with box joints rather than dovetails because Schrum found the look more in keeping with the chest's overall design.

An upholstered top provides color and soft contours while making a comfortable place to sit. The cushion involved no sewing, just foam batting, fabric, and staples. Fabric is wrapped around the edges of a piece of ½-in. plywood, which is then attached with screws from below. Screws sit in decorative ferrules.

The case is joined with a tool that's gaining ground with some furniture makers, the Festool Domino. Although expensive, the tool cuts mortises for small floating tenons very quickly and makes a joint like a biscuit joiner, only stronger. She also used standard biscuits in some places to align parts.

(CONTINUED)

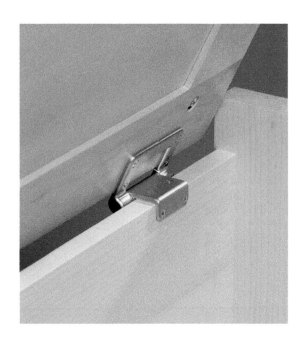

OPPOSITE Libby Schrum made this chest with solid maple and quartersawn maple veneer over plywood. The upholstered top adds color and texture.

ABOVE Torsion hinge lid supports from Rockler prevent the lid from slamming down. The upholstered top is attached to the lid with screws and decorative guitar ferrules, one of which is just visible to the right of the hinge.

Schrum does all of her designs in an Adobe℠ software program called Design Illustrator, which allows her to create the plan along with side and front views and to use different layers to add joinery or other details. She often follows that with a model to see how the piece will come together in three dimensions. In this case, it wasn't necessary. ▪

The main storage compartment is augmented with two spacious drawers at the bottom of the chest, which pull out on low-profile Accuride® slides.

Contemporary Design, Contemporary Assembly

The principal joinery in this maple chest by Libby Schrum is manufactured floating tenons whose mortises are made with a Festool Domino machine. The top, bottom, and intermediate divider are frame-and-panel assemblies.

FRONT

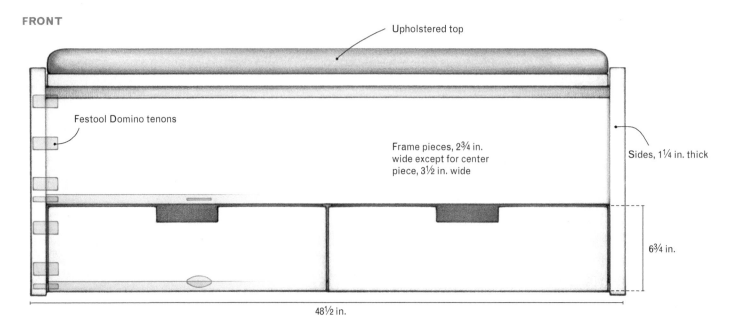

Upholstered top

Festool Domino tenons

Frame pieces, 2¾ in. wide except for center piece, 3½ in. wide

Sides, 1¼ in. thick

6¾ in.

48½ in.

SIDE

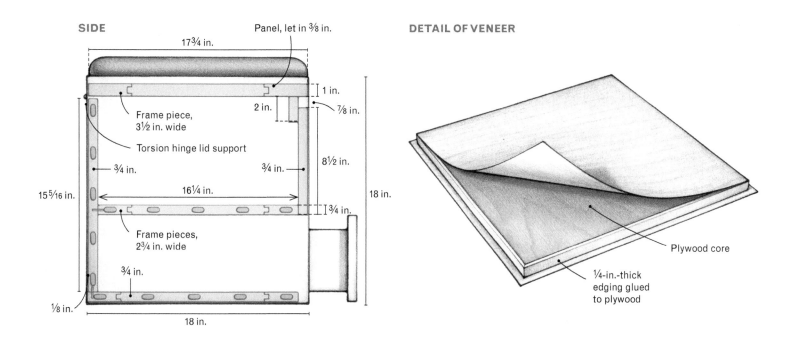

Panel, let in ⅜ in.

17¾ in.

1 in.

2 in.

⅞ in.

Frame piece, 3½ in. wide

Torsion hinge lid support

¾ in.

¾ in.

8½ in.

15⁵⁄₁₆ in.

16¼ in.

18 in.

¾ in.

Frame pieces, 2¾ in. wide

¾ in.

⅛ in.

18 in.

DETAIL OF VENEER

Plywood core

¼-in.-thick edging glued to plywood

Other than the frame-and-panel lid and interior dividers, the chest is made from veneered components. Schrum glued ¼-in.-thick edge-banding to plywood cores, then flushed the surfaces before veneer was pressed on the other side.

DRAWER FRONT

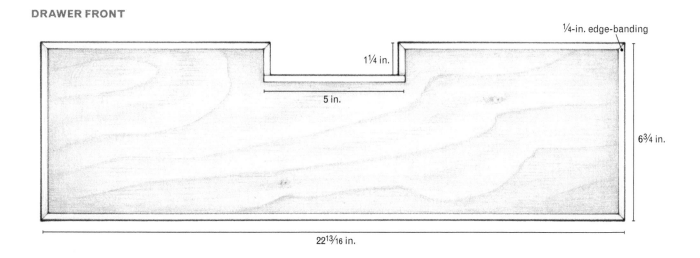

¼-in. edge-banding

1¼ in.

5 in.

6¾ in.

22¹³⁄₁₆ in.

INSTALLING TORSION HINGES

Rockler Woodworking and Hardware's℠ Torsion Hinge Lid Supports safely hold a chest lid at any position, eliminating the need for a separate lid stay.

Rockler's installation instructions recommend the hinge be surface mounted on the top back edge of the chest, which means there will be a ⅛-in. gap between the lid and the chest when the lid is closed. An alternative, worked out by Peter Turner, is to recess the body of the hinge in a shallow mortise. When the lid is closed, there is virtually no gap between the chest and the lid.

For this procedure, set the depth of cut just slightly less than the thickness of the hinge body where it saddles the back edge.

Clamp a stop at the end of the chest to guide the router and an extra piece of material on the back of the chest to prevent tearout (photo 1). Tape a shim (here a piece of blue card stock) to the stop, then make the first pass with the router to cut one end of the hinge mortise. Remove the shim and make a second pass to remove any burn marks.

1. A block of wood clamped to the back of the chest prevents tearout.

2. The distance between the edge of the router base and the bit helps determine the size of the block for the second pass.

3. With the block in place, cut a second groove, add the shim, and make another pass to remove burn marks.

Measure the distance between the edge of the router that rides against the stop and the router bit *(photo 2)*. Using this dimension, add a block to the original stop so the width of the mortise will be the width of the hinge body when closed plus ⅜ in. Cut the far end of the mortise, riding the router base against the block *(photo 3)*. Insert the shim and make a second pass.

Now you have defined the two edges of the mortise *(photo 4)*. Hog out the material between the two *(photo 5)*, and clean up the bottom of the mortise with a chisel or scraper and sandpaper *(photo 6)*.

Clamp a piece of material to the side of the chest to form a shelf to support the lid *(photo 7)*. Altering the thickness of the shim between the lid (represented in this photo by the board) and the back of the case will change the overhang of the lid when it's closed.

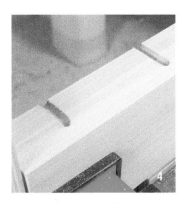

4. The small radius made by the router bit makes an attractive transition for the mortise.

5. With both ends cut, remove the material in the middle.

6. Clean up the mill marks with a chisel, scraper, and sandpaper.

7. Clamp a piece of wood to the chest to support the lid while attaching it.

The Un-Chest

A five-sided box with integral lid

ROBERT SCHULTZ
Kimberly, Wisconsin

DIMENSIONS	MATERIALS	HARDWARE	FINISH
33 in. wide, 24 in. deep, 30 in. high	Walnut	Brass mortise lock, casters, brass butt hinges	Minwax® wipe-on poly

Robert Schultz built the forerunner for this pyramid-shaped chest more than 40 years ago, near the very beginning of his woodworking career. He came up with the idea while looking for an alternative to the blanket chest of our forebears, the six-sided box.

The chest's front and back pieces slope inward to meet at a sharp peak, eliminating a conventional lid. The peak, in fact, is the lid, folding back to rest on the back of the case and allowing access to the storage space within. The bottom is a 3/8-in. panel let into grooves in the sides.

"The chest has Shaker simplicity and it seems to call for exposed joinery," says Schultz, a retired shop teacher. That was fine, too, but in addition to working out all the other construction details for this chest without a lid, Schultz also had to figure out how to cut dovetails. He'd never done that before.

Since that time, he's made three other chests like it. Along the way, Schultz learned to modify the dovetails along the angled edge to reduce the amount of short grain and improve strength. Instead of laying them out using the angled side as a reference point, he drew them at a 1:5 angle from an imaginary plumb line at the side of the case.

Sizing the chest, Schultz says, was critical. With an overall height of 30 in., both the front and back pieces are 32½ in. wide, a lot to manage when you're edge-gluing the blanks, and the chest is about as big as most bedrooms could accommodate. At 33 in. wide, the chest seemed to have the right proportions, although nowhere near the dimensions the "golden mean"—a 1.61 ratio of width to height—would have produced.

The triangular side pieces, as well as the front and back, are solid lumber. Because they are of different widths, Schultz wondered whether the wood's seasonal movement would eventually cause a problem as the pieces pushed and pulled against each other unevenly.

"Forty plus years have shown that concern not to be an issue, although I don't know why," Schultz says of his original case. "There is no warping of the chest or any changes at all with humidity. Maybe the cuts for the lid help to relieve the stress in whatever movement must take place."

Planning is one thing, doing another. To ensure a perfect fit, the lid was sliced from the top of the box after the case had been glued together. Schultz accomplished that with a combination of tablesaw and handsaw, but not without some careful planning.

(CONTINUED)

ABOVE Robert Schultz's efforts to build a chest unconventional in design led him to this steeply angled, five-sided box. He made the first of its kind more than 40 years ago when he first took up woodworking.

OPPOSITE The case is glued up first, then the top is sliced off to form the lid. Hinged at the back, the back of the lid comes to rest on the back of the case when opened and does not require a separate lid stay.

Gluing the case also had its challenges. The two ends were glued up as a single piece, then cut into triangular sections. Gluing the ends and front and back together was straightforward enough with pipe clamps, but that wouldn't work when it came time to clamp the triangular-shaped ridge. Instead of gluing blocks directly to the case to catch the clamps, Schultz glued on a layer of paper, then the cauls. The bond was strong enough to allow the clamps to pull the assembly together, but relatively easy to break later. ■

The Un-Chest

The front and back of this chest meet at a point and form the lid. The case is assembled first, then the lid is cut away. When the lid folds back, it stops against the back of the case and eliminates the need for a separate lid stay.

FRONT

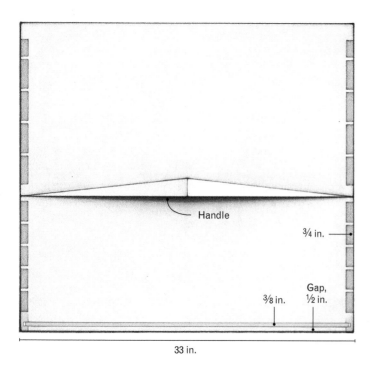

Handle

¾ in.

Gap, ½ in.

⅜ in.

33 in.

SIDE

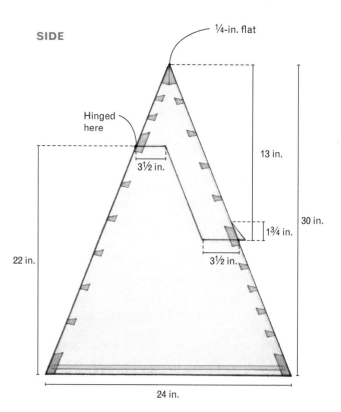

¼-in. flat

Hinged here

3½ in.

13 in.

1¾ in.

3½ in.

30 in.

22 in.

24 in.

TOP DETAIL

¼-in. flat

Dovetail angle
1:5 from plumb
line

¾ in.

BOTTOM CORNER DETAIL

³⁄₁₆ in. for
expansion

⅜ in.

½ in.

Ends of groove filled
after assembly

CUTTING OFF THE TOP

Cutting the top of the chest off to make the lid was a challenge. Before gluing up the case, Schultz made a mid-panel cut in each end piece (the horizontal cut in the photographs). After the case was assembled, he made two passes on the tablesaw to separate the lid, with the blade set at an angle *(photo 1)*. He finished the cuts with a backsaw *(photo 2)*.

Chest of Blankets

Recreating the soft fold of fabric in wood

RICHARD VAUGHAN
Queensland, Australia

DIMENSIONS	MATERIALS	HARDWARE	FINISH
21 in. deep, 32½ in. wide, 22 in. high	Tasmanian myrtle, Huon pine, marine plywood	Brass butt hinges, Stabilus® weight-balanced lid stay	Feast Watson® Floorseal® (polyurethane/tung oil blend), buffing oil

What better material to use for building a blanket chest than blankets, or at least wood that's been carved to look like blankets? With its softly contoured corners and a lid whose edges have been shaped to look like a folded blanket, Richard Vaughan's chest is not unlike the carved "linenfold" panels that first decorated European furniture and interiors centuries ago.

"I had the notion of a box made of blankets pretty well as soon as I was asked to make a blanket chest," Vaughan says. "I think of blankets as softly enclosing and concealing where dreams wait."

Vaughan is a professional furniture maker in Queensland, Australia, who has taught at the Center for Furniture Craftsmanship in Rockport, Maine. "My memory of my time in Maine early in 2009 holds the wonder of the way that a blanket of snow transforms terrain into contours. It makes a strong impression on someone who lives in a subtropical part of Australia. That memory takes me back 35 years to a winter I spent working in the north of Manitoba, near the Arctic circle. The gentle curves in that expanse of deep blanketing snow and the diamond dust sparkles when snowshoeing were utter magic."

OPPOSITE Richard Vaughan carved the edge of the top and sections of the base to suggest softly folded blankets. The chest is made from Tasmanian myrtle.

ABOVE Inside the chest is a lift-out tray with generously sized handles on each end. The bottom of the tray is unfinished Huon pine.

The chest is made from Tasmanian myrtle, in keeping with Vaughan's habit of using Australian hardwoods almost exclusively in his work. All of the wood making up the case sides is oriented with the grain running vertically, so the box shrinks and expands as a whole with changes in humidity. There's no cross-grain construction fighting itself.

Vaughan used 1^9/$_{16}$-in. material for sections of the chest that would be carved, and 1^1/$_{16}$-in. material in between so no gluelines would mar the carvings.

In arriving at his final design, Vaughan played with different blanket arrangements, photographed the ones he liked, and then did some sketching. In time, he modeled the chest in clay at a scale of 1:5 and then took the design to full-scale drawings. He practiced carving the folds and drapes of fabric in hoop pine, an inexpensive species, before diving into the real thing.

Once the myrtle box was glued up and marked for rough shaping, Vaughan went to work with three different grinders and then hand tools to form the blanket-like draping. The ends of the lid are carved to look like folds of fabric.

(CONTINUED)

PREVENTING CUP

Although Vaughan made the top from quartersawn boards to minimize the risk of cupping, he added a length of aluminum stock at each end for good measure. The lines between individual boards that make up edges of the lid are disguised by careful color matching and carving.

The bottom of the box is made from ¼-in. marine plywood faced with ⅛-in. myrtle. It's set in grooves in the case sides and prevented from shifting around by compressive foam. The bottom of the tray is ply faced with Huon pine, which Vaughan says has a distinctive fragrance and naturally repels insects. It's left unfinished.

Hinges for the lid were modified to allow the box to shrink and expand seasonally. Working with standard butt hinges, Vaughan cut back the ends of the barrels so the leaves screwed to the case would be able to move without affecting those screwed to the lid. He also reinforced the lid with aluminum angle stock, concealed in the ends, so it wouldn't cup. ▪

Gluing Up the Lid

Vaughan built the chest's lid by stacking boards all cut from one panel at the perimeter and then carving in a profile to resemble a folded blanket. A length of aluminum angle hidden in each end helps prevent the top from cupping.

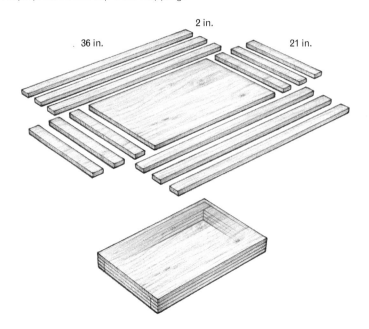

2 in.

36 in.

21 in.

Chest of Blankets

Richard Vaughan edge-glued pieces of Tasmanian myrtle together to form the body of his blanket chest before carving in contours to suggest folded fabric. At the corners and in the center of the front and back are thicker pieces of material so gluelines would not appear in the carving.

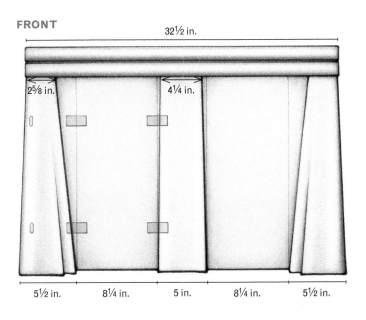

FRONT

32½ in.

2⅝ in.　　4¼ in.

5½ in.　　8¼ in.　　5 in.　　8¼ in.　　5½ in.

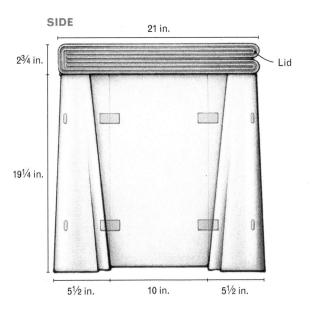

SIDE

21 in.

2¾ in.　　Lid

19¼ in.

5½ in.　　10 in.　　5½ in.

Case Assembly

The case is made from boards dressed to 1⁹⁄₁₆ in. and 1¹⁄₁₆ in. and edge-glued using Festool Domino tenons for accurate alignment. Vaughan carved the thicker pieces of material to look like draped fabric.

Festool Domino tenons

Thicker pieces for carving

Dogwood Blanket Chest

Intricate surface design, simplified construction

CRAIG THIBODEAU
San Diego, California

DIMENSIONS	MATERIALS	HARDWARE	FINISH
17⅛ in. deep, 34⅜ in. wide, 23¾ in. high	Solid mahogany; veneers of curly sycamore, dyed poplar, holly, and sapele; mother of pearl	Brass hinges and lid stay	Satin lacquer

C raig Thibodeau is giving us a look out the garden window at a blossoming dogwood tree. A window muntin bisects the scene and the left edge of the window frame abruptly cuts off our view. If we craned our necks just a bit, wouldn't we see the tree's main trunk?

The artful arrangement of curly sycamore, dyed poplar, and holly veneers, along with a mother-of-pearl butterfly, helps create the illusion. The asymmetrical view gives the marquetry an energy that a dogwood blossom perfectly centered in the chest's front panels would lack.

The dogwood motif is one Thibodeau has used before. "I have used the dogwood flower marquetry on four or five pieces now for a couple of reasons," he says. "I like how the flowers look and they are relatively quick to make, having only five or six pieces for each flower. One of the first marquetry pieces I made had a very simple version of the dogwood flowers and I have wavered back and forth between making the imagery more complex and then making it simpler again."

Veneers are stacked in a sandwich and cut with a scrollsaw (see the sidebar on pp. 70–71). Some pieces are scorched in hot sand to help create a three-dimensional look. Not surprising, Thibodeau has studied under two marquetry masters, Paul Schürch and Patrick Edwards, both of whom also have shops in California, and admires the work of the Art Deco designer Emile Jacques Ruhlmann.

There is something else going on here, though, and that is the elegantly detailed cabinet work. It could be a touch of James Krenov, whose "attention to the finest details of a piece" has great appeal for Thibodeau.

Thibodeau is in complete control of the process. He begins by laying up the plywood cores for the top, sides, and bottom of the chest from lightweight poplar plywood: two pieces of 1/2-in. material for everything but the curved front panels. Those are laminated from six layers of 1/8-in. plywood before they are veneered. The inside of the case is veneered completely in sapele.

When it comes to joinery, Thibodeau is looking for efficiency as well as strength. "My methods have changed a bit since I started," he says, "with the primary change being additional speed at each step of the process. Since I do this for a living, time is money and anywhere I can save time helps."

The legs are glued to the side panels with 1/8-in.-thick by 1-in.-wide splines that are let into the panels and the legs in stopped grooves. The bottom of the chest is dadoed into the front and back panels and also secured with splines. The same goes for the connections between the sides of the chest and the bottom.

(CONTINUED)

OPPOSITE Craig Thibodeau used veneers of curly sycamore, dyed poplar, and holly to create this picture of a blossoming dogwood tree. Like window muntins, the mahogany frame defines the view.

ABOVE One reason Thibodeau likes the dogwood flower is that each blossom requires only a half-dozen pieces, somewhat simplifying the marquetry. Gently scorching the edges of the veneered petals in hot sand provides shading and a three-dimensional look.

The Festool Domino machine, which cuts mortises for loose tenons in roughly the same way as a biscuit joiner, has been a real boon. It has replaced a router jig that had to be tailored for each joint, allowing very accurate placement and high strength. Those connections join legs to the upper and lower stretchers on the front and back.

Thibodeau usually does much of his design work with computer software, but only to get a "rough shape" and a starting point for the project. He says he frequently modifies the design as he works. In this case, for example, he added more curvature to the stretchers along with a center divider on the front panel after the chest was underway. Several mother-of-pearl butterflies on the top also were changes made on the fly. ∎

Chest Joinery

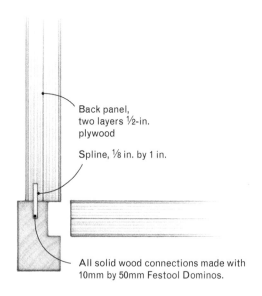

Back panel, two layers ½-in. plywood

Spline, ⅛ in. by 1 in.

All solid wood connections made with 10mm by 50mm Festool Dominos.

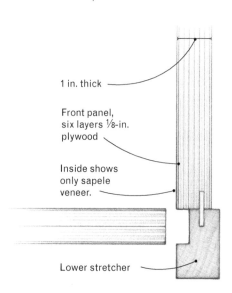

1 in. thick

Front panel, six layers ⅛-in. plywood

Inside shows only sapele veneer.

Lower stretcher

Dogwood Blanket Chest

Craig Thibodeau lays up the substrate for the veneer panels from poplar plywood, two pieces of ½-in. material for the sides, top, and bottom, and six pieces of ⅛-in. material for the curved front panels. He starts each design with computer modeling software. The top is made from two layers of ⅜-in. plywood.

TOP

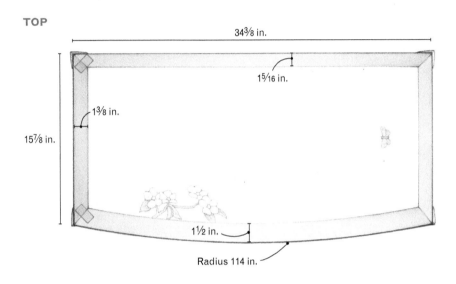

FRONT

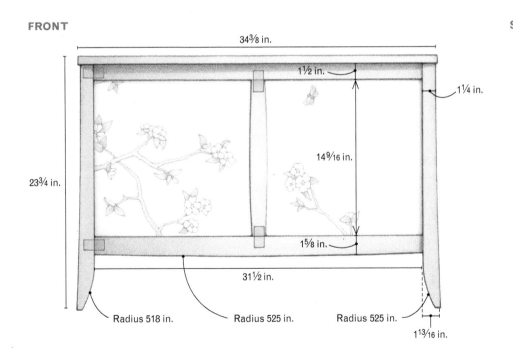

SIDE

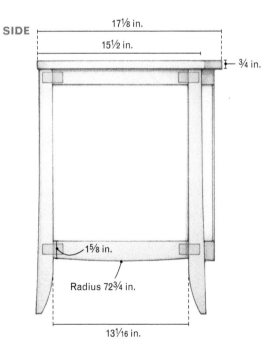

A COMPLETE PICTURE FROM ONE SERIES OF CUTS

Craig Thibodeau creates an image of a flowering dogwood tree by assembling a stack of veneers and cutting all of the pieces at the same time. An extremely thin blade virtually eliminates a saw kerf, so that the same cut creating a void in the background veneer simultaneously creates the colored veneer that will fill it.

Start by drawing the design and selecting veneers that will be used for the background and the other parts of the design. Spray-glue a copy of the drawing to a piece of stiff card stock, and tape the background veneer to another piece of card stock the same size *(photo 1)*.

Tape pieces of colored veneer over the background so their position corresponds with the drawing. That is, brown pieces of veneer are taped in the area where a tree branch will appear; pieces of green veneer go where leaves will appear. Orient the grain of the veneer to follow the natural flow in the drawing.

Once all of the pieces are taped down, tape the card stock with the drawing to the top of the pile to create a single packet.

Now it's time to cut the pieces with a scrollsaw *(photo 2)*. As each section is cut away from the packet, place it to the side.

1. Tape small pieces of colored veneer on the background veneer, locating them so they correspond with details in the drawing. The background veneer (in this case, curly sycamore) has been taped to a piece of card stock. The drawing is spray-glued to an identically sized piece of card stock.

2. Place the drawing over the package of veneers, tape the two layers together, and begin cutting out the pieces with a scrollsaw. Thibodeau is using a 2/0 blade. As each component is cut free, gently remove it and set it aside.

Putting the pieces over a second copy of the drawing will help to keep them from getting mixed up.

Once all the pieces have been cut, remove the background from the packet and cover the back side with blue painter's tape. Now, flip the background over and insert the pieces of the picture into the background one at a time.

Shading can make the picture more realistic *(photo 3)*. Heat some fine sand over a hot plate (set on medium), then, one at a time, dip in the edges of pieces you want to shade. Don't leave the veneer pieces in the sand for too long. Lightly moisten each piece with clean water and place into the taped background.

Cover the top of the picture with blue painter's tape (use the kind with a 60-day release), remove the tape from the back, and the veneer is ready to glue down to the substrate.

3. Apply blue painter's tape to the back of the field piece, then begin applying pieces of the marquetry image. Fine sand heated over medium heat on a hot plate shades veneer edges.

A Chest for Work

Unusual request, unusual design

TERRY MOORE
Wilmot, New Hampshire

DIMENSIONS
18 in. deep, 36 in. wide,
18 in. high

MATERIALS
Fiddleback makore veneer,
ebony, mahogany,
medium-density fiberboard,
western red cedar,
quartersawn white oak

HARDWARE
Brass butt hinges and door
catch

FINISH
Catalyzed lacquer

The commission was for a chest, but the customer had no plans to use it for sweaters, blankets, quilts, linens, or any of the other things that usually go into a piece of furniture like this. This is a writing chest, designed as a birthday present for a businessman who preferred to conduct his affairs from the comfort of an easy chair. And what he needed was a chest that could be parked next to the chair like an end table, something that would keep papers and office supplies organized and give him a place to park his laptop computer. From his chair, the owner could easily reach into the three drawers that slide from one end of the chest. On one long face, a swinging door opens to a shelf; the other door is a dummy that conceals the drawer runners.

"I think what excited me about the piece was its original brief," says Terry Moore. "I have never seen anything quite like this before. I also love to make well-fitting hand-dovetailed drawers, and this gave me an opportunity to have some fun and show off a little."

Moore says the owner is an avid collector of Federal period furniture, so the chest had to be traditional in appearance. That helped Moore come up with the curved bottom rail of the base and no doubt contributed to some of the other details. "Clean lines, beautiful veneer, ebony inlays, high-quality finish, and well-fitted drawers are all hallmarks of what I do best," he says. The inlaid compass rose in the middle of the top seemed appropriate for someone who owns a house on the ocean. The chest gets a lot of its impact from the heavily figured veneer, a hallmark of Moore's work and also of the French Art Deco movement with which Moore was once enamored.

Moore is a self-taught professional who has been making furniture full time since 1976, so construction of this chest seemed routine despite the technical difficulties it presented.

Given the exactness of design and execution, it's surprising to learn that Moore is accustomed to making a lot of it up as he goes. He works from rough sketches only and builds no prototypes. Moore says he began with general information about the piece, such as overall dimensions, but worked out the details as he made the chest. For example, it wasn't entirely clear how the dummy door or the concealed drawer runners would be built when he started. But those and other details presented themselves as he worked. "It's much like writing music," he says. ▪

OPPOSITE Terry Moore's chest in makore veneer was designed for a businessman as a work station that could be placed next to an easy chair. Some of the details are derived from the Federal period, a particular interest of the owner.

A Chest for Work

Terry Moore's veneered chest is really an office work center with three drawers and a storage compartment. The back and left side are made with ¾-in. ultralight MDF veneered with fiddleback makore. All edges are mitered and joined with small biscuits.

TOP

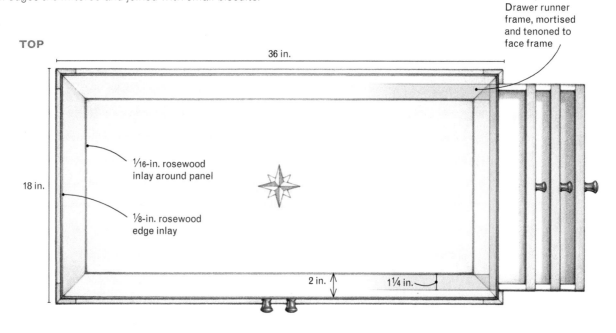

Drawer runner frame, mortised and tenoned to face frame

36 in.

18 in.

¹⁄₁₆-in. rosewood inlay around panel

⅛-in. rosewood edge inlay

2 in.

1¼ in.

FRONT

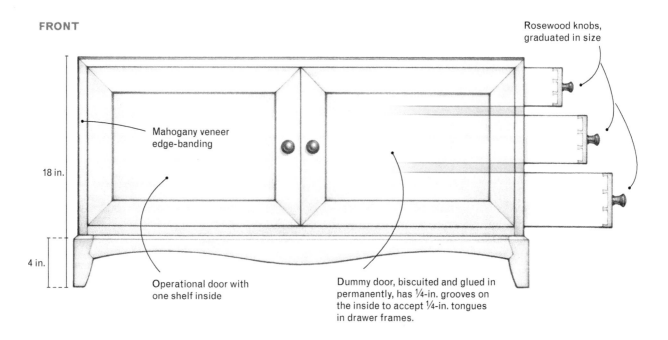

Rosewood knobs, graduated in size

Mahogany veneer edge-banding

18 in.

4 in.

Operational door with one shelf inside

Dummy door, biscuited and glued in permanently, has ¼-in. grooves on the inside to accept ¼-in. tongues in drawer frames.

One door opens for storage, and the other is a dummy that conceals the runners for a bank of drawers.

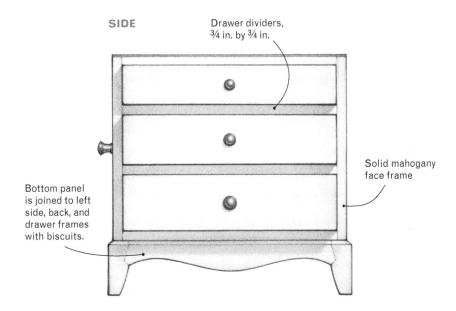

SIDE

Drawer dividers, ¾ in. by ¾ in.

Bottom panel is joined to left side, back, and drawer frames with biscuits.

Solid mahogany face frame

Little House

Bold surface carved at breakneck speed

PETER PIEROBON
Vancouver, British Columbia, Canada

DIMENSIONS
22 in. deep, 44 in. wide,
32 in. high

MATERIALS
Cherry

HARDWARE
Brass hinges and lid stay

FINISH
Aniline dye, clear lacquer

W ith its peaked lid and gable ends, Peter Pierobon's chest might pass for a diminutive house, and in fact the idea of a house-like shape for personal storage is what motivated the design. But it is the deeply textured exterior surface that gives the chest its energy.

The chest is one of a pair that Pierobon built at the same time. The first is decorated with a pattern of raised shapes spread over the surface, similar to other Pierobon designs that use decorative glyphs derived from text (Gregg shorthand is one familiar Pierobon motif).

He found the first chest "incredibly time consuming, almost two months start to finish." So when it came time to complete the second one he was ready for a little spontaneity.

"In response to the first box I decided to take this one out on the sidewalk and complete the surface carving in one day," he says. Pierobon did some sample carving in preparation, but he didn't really know what the finished result would be, and he realized he was putting the entire project at risk. If the carving didn't work out, for whatever the reason, the chest would be ruined.

He attacked the surface with just about everything he had on hand: a modified Lamello® biscuit joiner, carving gouges, a grinder, and even a chainsaw. It was a big plunge for a furniture maker who in the past worked strictly from full-scale drawings and scale models.

"That is how I worked for the first half of my career," he says. "I now make much more sculptural work and use scale models to resolve the piece, only drawing full-size details if necessary for joinery."

In the end, he was happy with the result. The deep furrows, colored with aniline dye to a uniform black, contrast sharply with the warm glow of the chest's natural cherry interior.

Pierobon returned to his hometown of Vancouver in 2000 after a number of career stops in the United States, starting with four years with Wendell Castle—two as a student and another two as an employee in Castle's shop. Castle, arguably the most influential studio furniture maker in the United States, remains an important mentor.

Pierobon also taught at the University of the Arts in Philadelphia and at the California College of Arts and Crafts. He was a founder of the Furniture Society. ▪

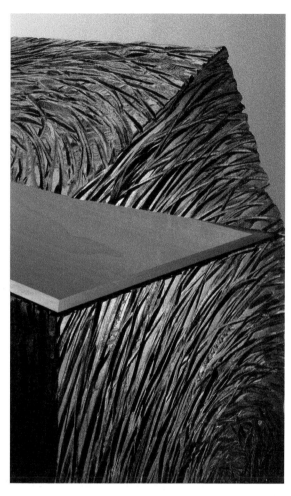

OPPOSITE The exterior of Peter Pierobon's chest is dominated by the swirling pattern of its carved surface. Pierobon did the carving in a single day with tools that included a modified biscuit joiner and a chainsaw.

ABOVE The natural cherry of the chest interior glows warmly, a sharp contrast to the textured black exterior.

TWO APPROACHES,
TWO CHESTS

Peter Pierobon built two chests at roughly the same time, both of which featured dramatic surface carving. But as he explains, they were entirely different in some important ways:

"They really were a pair and expressed two completely different approaches to designing and working. *Dark Thoughts* (pictured here) was the first to be conceived and executed, taking many weeks of laborious carving and sanding to finish. My focus, commitment, and fingertips were all compromised by the end of this project. When it came to tackling *Van Gogh's Box* I decided to take a much riskier approach. After making samples of various textures using a variety of tools, both hand and power, I literally attacked the box with no preconceived understanding of how it would unfold. This process is quite similar to sketching with a pencil on a piece of paper except the potential loss is much greater if it fails."

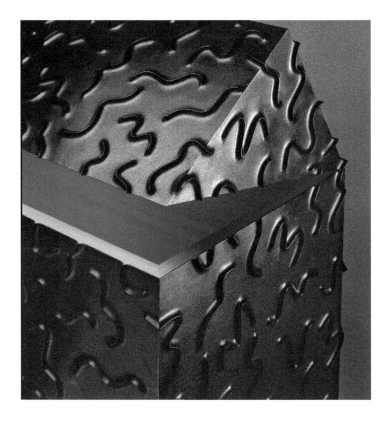

Little House

Peter Pierobon's house-like storage chest is made with splined miter corners and a deeply textured exterior surface. Case sides are made with 8/4 material that has been milled to 1½ in. to allow enough material for surface carving.

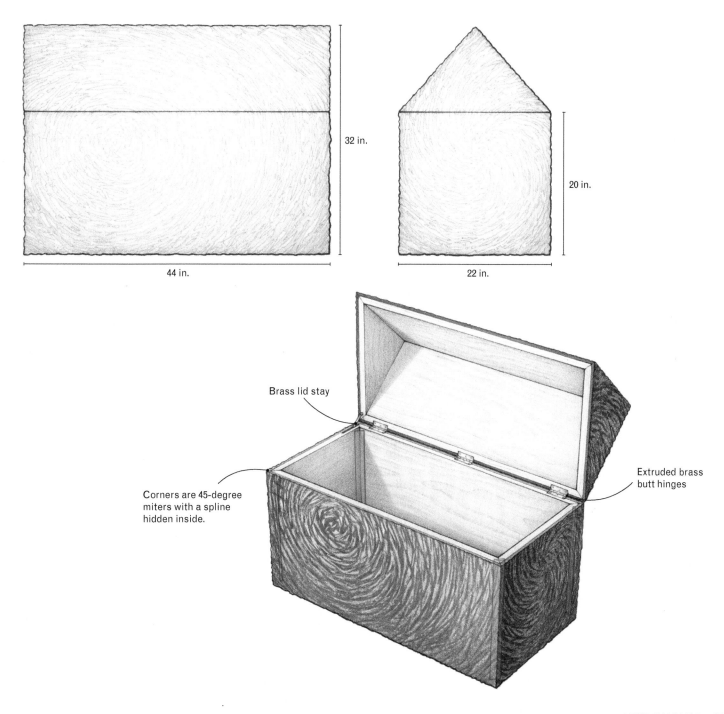

32 in.

44 in.

20 in.

22 in.

Brass lid stay

Corners are 45-degree miters with a spline hidden inside.

Extruded brass butt hinges

Sea Chest

Above and below the surface

MITCH RYERSON
Cambridge, Massachusetts

DIMENSIONS	MATERIALS	HARDWARE	FINISH
15 in. deep, 40½ in. wide, 18½ in. high	Old-growth Douglas fir, anigré, Swiss pear, aromatic cedar, Baltic birch plywood	Brass cabinet hinges	General Finishes® Arm-R-Seal

Trained at Boston University's Program in Artisanry, Mitch Ryerson has been a furniture maker for more than 27 years, and there have been some changes along the way. "I started out very conservatively as a designer," he says, "then I got very interested in color and narrative work. Now I am again very interested in natural wood and in simpler forms."

This sea chest, commissioned by someone who loves to sail, seems to embody all of those influences. Its natural wood components are a mix of old-growth Douglas fir for the frame and Swiss pear for both the top and the brackets for the rope handles. The panel molding is figured anigré, an African hardwood, and the chest bottom is aromatic cedar.

Ryerson chose the woods because they were close in color value and made what he called a "gentle palette" without jarring contrasts. He's balanced the warm hues of the natural wood with brightly decorated panels on the sides of the case and oversize rope handles on the ends.

The panels are ½-in. Baltic birch plywood finished in a design that evokes the movement of water or aquatic plant life swaying in a gentle current. Ryerson got the effect by using two layers of glaze, yellow first followed by phthalocyanine blue. The translucent colors mix to become a swirl of yellow, green, and blue. Ryerson says one advantage of using glazes is that they dry more slowly than paint, so they can be worked after they are applied. This surface, he says, is "basic finger painting." (For how he did it, see pp. 84–85.)

The top of the chest is a slice of ocean, the peaks of the waves rising ¾ in. in height from the troughs; the entire surface was chip carved with a series of indentations to mimic the surface of the ocean beaten by rain or ruffled by wind.

Pear is a dense, fine-grained wood that's ideal for carving. Ryerson roughed out the shape of the waves with a router, then planed across the grain in from either edge to refine the shape. A spokeshave helped him get the final contours, but he left the surface ⅛ in. higher than the finished surface to allow for the carving.

The indentations are made with a very sharp gouge going cross-grain, a technique that produces a clean cut as long as the tool is sharp enough. In the end, the surface has a pleasing texture and is a comfortable seat.

The rope handles are traditional "beckets," as they are called, made by Tim Whitten in Stonington, Maine. In a process adapted from an old rope treatment called "worm, parcel, and serve," Whitten wraps canvas over a core of rope, snugs that up with a wrapping of twine, and finishes each

(CONTINUED)

OPPOSITE Mitch Ryerson's sea chest combines a range of woods in muted tones with boldly decorated panels and a lid that suggests the motion of the sea.

Sea Chest

This frame-and-panel chest has a carved lid suggesting the rippled surface of the ocean and glazed panels that could be undersea plant life. The bottom is made from planks of aromatic cedar set on a ledger.

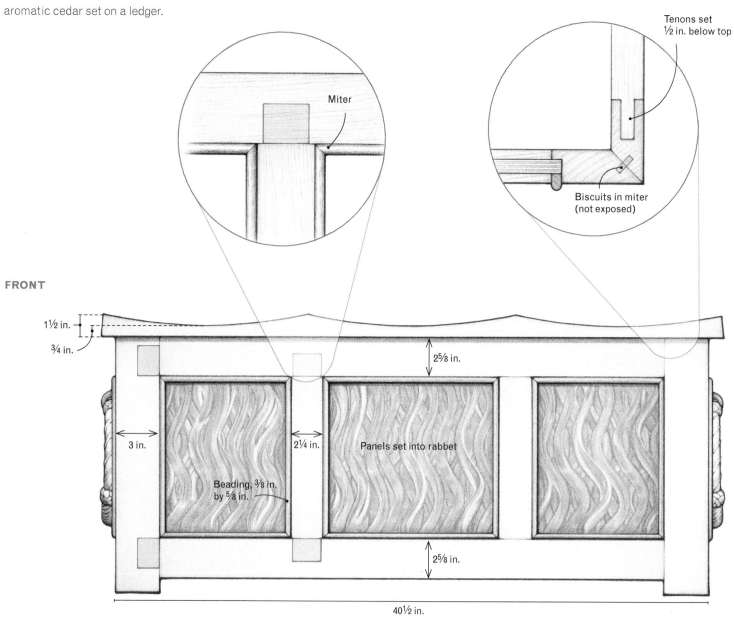

Tenons set ½ in. below top

Miter

Biscuits in miter (not exposed)

FRONT

1½ in.

¾ in.

2⅝ in.

3 in.

2¼ in.

Panels set into rabbet

Beading, ⅜ in. by ⅝ in.

2⅝ in.

40½ in.

handle with traditional Turk's head knots (see the sidebar on pp. 86–87). Sailors at sea made beckets with the same set of skills they used to make and repair sails and rigging, Whitten says. These beckets, believe it or not, represent very basic skills.

"I was not sure how well the rope work would go with the rest of the chest," Ryerson says. "I was pleasantly surprised with how it all works together." ■

SIDE

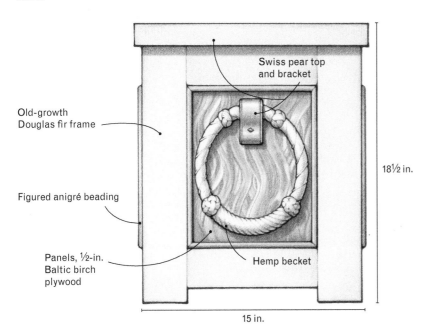

Swiss pear top and bracket

Old-growth Douglas fir frame

Figured anigré beading

Panels, ½-in. Baltic birch plywood

Hemp becket

18½ in.

15 in.

MAKING GLAZED PANELS

Mitch Ryerson's blanket chest incorporates panels that are painted and glazed in a multistep process that gives them an unusual visual depth.

He starts with slightly oversize pieces of ½-in. Baltic birch plywood and sands them to 220-grit. Any voids are filled with vinyl spackle, and the panels are sanded again with 220-grit paper.

Then Ryerson sprays on two coats of white alkyd primer, allowing one day between coats. After each coat, he sands with 220-grit paper and removes dust with a tack cloth.

Next is one coat of yellow Japan Color *(photo 1),* a flat paint with a very rich pigment content that has been thinned slightly and strained to remove any lumps before spraying *(photo 2).*

After the paint has dried for a day, Ryerson sands lightly with 220-grit paper *(photo 3)* and removes sanding dust with a tack cloth *(photo 4).* Then he applies one coat of thin shellac with a soft brush *(photo 5),* making continuous, smooth strokes from one end of the panel to the other. After that dries, he sands lightly with 220-grit paper and removes the sanding dust with a tack cloth. The base is now complete.

Ryerson makes his blue glaze by mixing roughly 3 tsp. of phthalo blue artist's oil to ½ in. of mineral spirits in a clean jar *(photo 6).* The thinner dissolves the oil thoroughly, and Ryerson then adds the colorless, oil-based glaze.

The blue glaze is applied over the painted panels with a broad artist's brush. The idea is to provide a smooth, even layer. He applies glaze first in a vertical pattern and then, with a relatively dry brush, evens out the field with horizontal strokes *(photo 7).*

One of the advantages of using the glaze is that it remains workable for up to 45 minutes, giving Ryerson plenty of time to

1. After priming, panels get a coat of yellow Japan color.

2. Paint is strained to remove any bits before spraying.

3. When the paint has dried, Ryerson sands lightly.

4. Sanding dust is removed with a tack cloth.

work the surface with gloved fingers into a pattern that looks like undulating undersea plants *(photo 8)*. The horizontal brush marks of the base are visible in places between the squiggles he's made with his fingers, as if you could look through the waving vegetation. The panels are not sanded after the application of the glaze.

The color of the surface varies with the thickness of the glaze, ranging from deep blue where none of the yellow peeks through to green in areas where both yellow and blue are visible.

After the glaze has dried for a couple of days, Ryerson sprays the surface with a coat of satin polyurethane and cuts the panels to their finished size. Both sides of the panels are treated the same so they react to moisture equally.

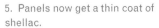

5. Panels now get a thin coat of shellac.

6. The blue glaze is made with artist's oil.

7. Panels get a smooth, even layer of glaze with a brush.

8. Fingers make the squiggles.

MAKING ROPE BECKETS

The handles for Mitch Ryerson's blanket chest, properly called beckets, were made by Tim Whitten, a craftsman in Stonington, Maine.

Beckets were traditionally woven from rope and made sturdy as well as decorative handles for sea chests. The techniques used to make them are derived from methods sailors developed to protect standing rigging from weather and decay. Whitten, who earned a PhD in mechanical engineering before turning to full-time rope work, scoured books, the Internet, and maritime museum collections to teach himself the craft.

Ryerson's beckets begin with a length of cotton rope. Although not as strong as hemp or manila, cotton is soft and easy to work with and more than strong enough for this use. Whitten begins by unraveling a bit of the rope at each end. He cuts a length of canvas that will be used to wrap the center section *(photo 1)* and folds and presses the edges with a wooden tool called a seam rubber *(photo 2)*. Then the canvas is folded around the rope and stitched in place *(photo 3)*.

When the center of the handle is encased in canvas, Whitten wraps it with twine, working the cord into the twist of the rope at

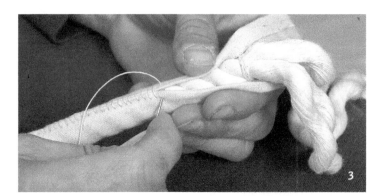

1. Tim Whitten starts with a length of cotton rope and measures off a narrow strip of canvas that will form its outer shell.

2. The edges of the canvas are folded over and creased with a wooden tool called a seam rubber. Whitten made this one from lignum vitae, a hard, dense wood.

3. The canvas is wrapped around the rope core and stitched closed with linen thread.

4. Cord applied over the line fills the grooves in the rope.

5. With the cord in place, Whitten uses a steel awl to pull one strand at a time taut.

6. Whitten starts an eye by separating the rope into a number of distinct strands.

first by hand and then tightening it with the help of a steel awl *(photos 4 and 5)*.

Now Whitten forms an eye at each end of the handle, which will be used to attach the becket to wood cleats on the chest with a decoratively capped bolt rope. Whitten separates the strands of rope at each end of the handle *(photo 6)* and makes a loop by overlapping several of them into a "Flemish eye" *(photo 7)*. Excess material is cut away *(photo 8)*. He wraps the eye in a length of cord to form a smooth, tight loop with no abrupt transitions *(photo 9)*. Working with a stout sailmaker's needle,

Whitten stitches a fancy pattern from the end of the canvas up and around the eye at each end *(photo 10)* to complete the handle.

This bolt rope is made from five equal lengths of twine. The center, the part that will pass through the cleat, is bound in cord *(photo 11)* and the ends are shaped into distinctive knobs *(photo 12)*.

There's a lot of maritime history and tradition in what Whitten does. "The more elaborate a sailor was able to construct a set of beckets, the more it spoke directly to his skills as a seaman," Whitten says. "Having a set of fancy sea chest beckets was sort of like having a good resume."

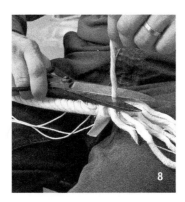

7. A few of the strands are formed into a Flemish eye and bound at the center with cord.

8. Excess material is cut away in such a way to create a smooth transition from the body of the becket to the eye.

9. Now the neck and eye of the becket can be wrapped with cord to make a smooth, tight core for fancy stitchwork that will follow.

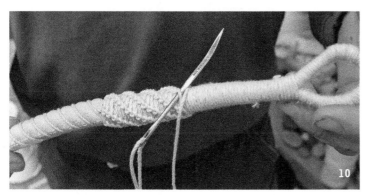

10. Fancy stitching starts from the end of the canvas wrapping and extends all the way around each eye.

11. The rope bolt is formed by five strands of cord, bound in the middle with a separate piece of twine.

12. A knob is formed on one end of the rope bolt. The rope will pass through the eyes of the beckets and the cleat attached to the chest. Once the becket is in place, Whitten makes the second knob that locks it in.

A Boat Builder's Chest

Lapstrake top curved like a ship's hull

EJLER HJORTH-WESTH
Elk, California

DIMENSIONS	MATERIALS	HARDWARE	FINISH
21 in. deep, 37⅞ in. wide, 21 in. high	Mahogany, Douglas fir, Port Orford cedar, Goncalo Alves (interior tray runners)	Brass butt hinges, chain lid support, lock	Shellac

We think of sea chests as the sturdy wooden boxes in which sailors stowed their gear while living aboard a ship. But Ejler Hjorth-Westh, who started his furniture-making career as a boatbuilding apprentice, has made a literal interpretation of this form with a chest lid built like the curved hull of a dory.

Hjorth-Westh built the chest as a student at the College of the Redwoods in northern California while studying under the late James Krenov. Certain elements were expected—frame-and-panel construction, dovetails, dowelling, and a shellac finish—whereas other parts of the design were a blank slate.

"This was my first project studying at Krenov's school," he says. "Coming from a background in boatbuilding, I wanted to incorporate something I knew intimately: lapstrake construction. It was also important that I build something I wanted to own myself, a significant piece of furniture, which could capture a place in the house but without bravado."

There are more curves and angles than may seem apparent at first. In addition to the domed lid, the case angles outward at 2½ degrees off plumb as it goes up, meaning that the panel boards making up the front of the chest are tapered as well. Consequently, the dovetails at the top of the case are angled, not square. Even the groove in the frame for the lid must be cut at an angle as well as a curve, what Hjorth-Westh describes as a "white-knuckled operation" he practiced on a mock-up first.

The lid is the most dominant visual element of the chest, a complicated piece of work. Hjorth-Westh starts with a mock-up frame that creates a pleasingly shaped dome. The individual strips, or "strakes," are laid out a pair at a time, beginning at the outermost edges. Each set gets a tapered rabbet to allow top and bottom surfaces at the ends of the lid to be flush while the center of the lid has a familiar lapstrake pattern.

When the lid is completely fabricated, it's removed from the frame, sized on the real frame, and then trimmed to size. In the completed top, the lapstrake lid fits in a groove cut all the way around the inside of the frame.

The panels making up the sides of the chest are no less involved. Panel boards are first rabbeted on adjoining faces, then cut to a taper and glued together. Staves, which are slightly proud of the surface, are cut to a taper to fit the grooves and glued in later.

(CONTINUED)

OPPOSITE Ejler Hjorth-Westh's interpretation of a traditional sea chest includes a lapstrake lid, reflecting the maker's apprenticeship as a boat builder before he turned to furniture.

ABOVE The ends of the curved lid form a flush surface so they can fit into a groove in the frame. But in midfield, the individual strakes take on the familiar pattern of a traditionally made wooden boat.

A Boat Builder's Chest

This chest has a tapered shape and a lapstrake top, details that substantially complicated its construction. The top, formed over a mock-up frame, is made by cutting tapered rabbets into the edges of individual strakes and fitting them one at a time.

FRONT

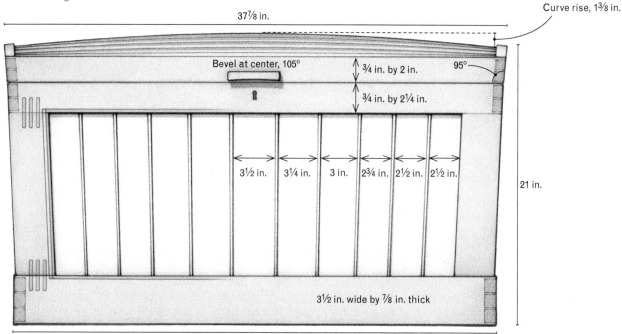

Curve rise, 1³⁄₈ in.

37⁷⁄₈ in.

Bevel at center, 105°

³⁄₄ in. by 2 in.

95°

³⁄₄ in. by 2¹⁄₄ in.

21 in.

3¹⁄₂ in.   3¹⁄₄ in.   3 in.   2³⁄₄ in.   2¹⁄₂ in.   2¹⁄₂ in.

3¹⁄₂ in. wide by ⁷⁄₈ in. thick

36¹⁄₂ in.

SIDE

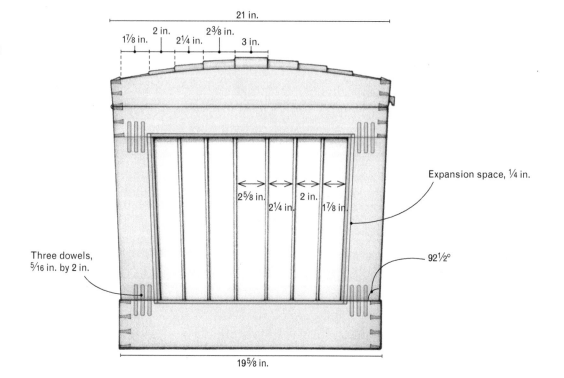

21 in.

1⁷⁄₈ in.   2 in.   2¹⁄₄ in.   2³⁄₈ in.   3 in.

Expansion space, ¹⁄₄ in.

2⁵⁄₈ in.   2¹⁄₄ in.   2 in.   1⁷⁄₈ in.

Three dowels, ⁵⁄₁₆ in. by 2 in.

92¹⁄₂°

19⁵⁄₈ in.

Hjorth-Westh says a number of ideas, some of them originating with his teachers, were "tried and discarded" before a final design emerged. Then, he adds, "Close the book, brother, time to build!"

The attention to the finest details certainly reflects the two years of study with Krenov, which Hjorth-Westh calls a "monumental experience." He says he continues to read Krenov's books and finds inspiration and a comforting familiarity in working with wood in the old ways, by hand.

"Whenever I open this chest, a cozy aroma greets me, of cedar and wool, that spells winter weather and weak light," he says. "But there is something more. We had a large chest in our house when I was a child. I think the feeling when opening a lid to a chest is a good, perhaps secret feeling. I guess it never goes away." ■

BOTTOM DETAIL

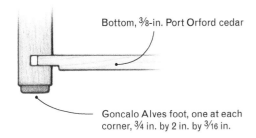

Bottom, ⅜-in. Port Orford cedar

Goncalo Alves foot, one at each corner, ¾ in. by 2 in. by ³⁄₁₆ in.

TRAY DETAIL

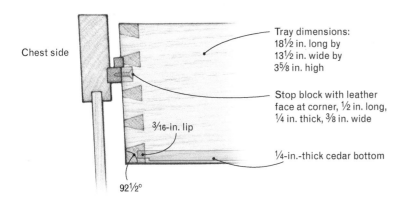

Chest side

Tray dimensions: 18½ in. long by 13½ in. wide by 3⅝ in. high

Stop block with leather face at corner, ½ in. long, ¼ in. thick, ⅜ in. wide

³⁄₁₆-in. lip

¼-in.-thick cedar bottom

92½°

Inside the mahogany and Douglas Fir chest is a tray that slides from side to side on a runner made from goncalo alves. Like the chest, the sides of the tray are tapered outward at 92½ degrees.

Flower Power

A new take on a very old furniture style

BRIAN REID
Rockland, Maine

DIMENSIONS	MATERIALS	HARDWARE	FINISH
25 in. deep, 52¾ in. wide, 35 in. high	Cherry, maple, various veneers	Brass lid stays	Nitrocellulose lacquer

Hadley chests, as they are called, are rare finds for collectors of early American furniture. Named for the Massachusetts town where Hartford collector Henry Wood Erving found one in the 19th century, the chests have largely disappeared. Only a few hundred still exist.

Boxy and solidly built, the chests were made for young women as part of their dowries, often incised with a tulip and leaf motif, their initials, and painted in bright colors: Prussian blue, red, black, and white. The chests typically had three panels across the front and a drawer at the bottom. They've been called the "Mercedes of American chests."

There are two Hadley-inspired chests in this book, including this one by Maine furniture maker Brian Reid (for the other example, see David Stenstrom's chest on p. 128). Like its historical antecedents, Reid's chest is brightly decorated, but with a pattern of veneered flowers instead of paint and incised carvings.

It may seem like an unlikely choice for Reid, who says his preferences bounce between Arts and Crafts and Modernism. But Reid, who studied under the English master John Makepeace at Parham College, has broad interests among designers. The list includes Ulrika Scriba, a German craftswoman who taught him parquetry, and the 18th-century French parquetry virtuoso Charles Andre Boulle.

Actually, Reid says, the flower motif has an equally varied history, ranging from Egyptian furniture to the hippie movement of the 1960s. It was Reid's goal to mimic the overall proportions of a Hadley chest but make the decorative pattern of his own design.

The idea of using a Hadley chest as the basis for the design came to Reid after he saw an original at Yale. He had just moved to Maine after 10 years in the Aspen, Colorado, area, and the thought of a smaller case piece with a solid New England pedigree seemed like a good idea.

Reid's marquetry panels are veneer over ¼-in. Baltic plywood set into a rabbeted frame. Panels are held in place by molding secured with copper nails.

Reid cuts the veneer flowers on a 1936 scrollsaw, stacking a dozen squares of different kinds of veneer together and cutting the design with a very fine-kerf blade. Once he has shuffled the pieces to distribute the different colors and reassembled them, he has both the flower petals and the field with a single cut. There are a total of four different flower patterns on the chest.

(CONTINUED)

OPPOSITE Brian Reid's chest is based on an early American design called the Hadley chest, named for a Connecticut River town in Massachusetts where they were made in the early 18th century.

ABOVE The chest's panels are veneer over ¼-in. plywood. Reid cuts the flower patterns out on a scrollsaw a dozen at a time. When the pieces are shuffled and reassembled, they create these contrasting patterns.

Flower Power

Brian Reid's cherry and veneer chest is modeled after the Hadley dowry chests of the early 18th century. Sturdy in construction, the frame-and-panel chests were originally decorated with incised carvings and bright paint.

FRONT

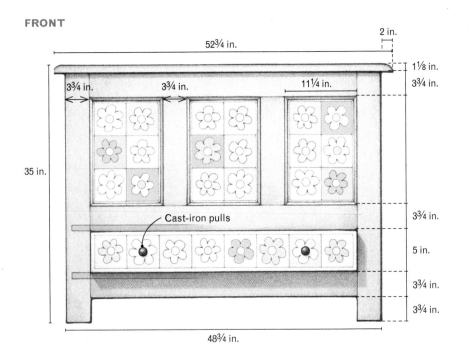

2 in.

52¾ in.

1⅛ in.

3¾ in.

3¾ in.

3¾ in.

11¼ in.

35 in.

3¾ in.

Cast-iron pulls

5 in.

3¾ in.

3¾ in.

48¾ in.

SIDE

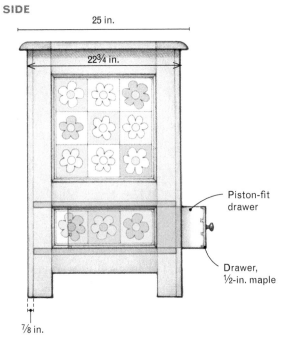

25 in.

22¾ in.

Piston-fit drawer

Drawer, ½-in. maple

⅞ in.

TOP

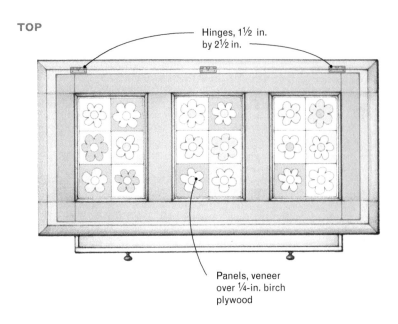

Hinges, 1½ in. by 2½ in.

Panels, veneer over ¼-in. birch plywood

He'd make two changes if he were to make the chest again. The first would be to use 12/4 material for the legs instead of following the traditional construction technique of joining flat frame-and-panel assemblies. The conventional way of joining the case creates L-shaped corners and unattractive seams where front and back panels meet the sides.

Reid also would shy away from the nitrocellulose lacquer he used here and choose an oil/varnish finish instead. Lacquer, he says, doesn't seem to age well and interferes with the rich reddish-brown patina that cherry should develop.

There's one other thing he'd do differently: make sure the door to the shop is securely latched. Reid, the senior fellow at the Center for Furniture Craftsmanship, says the top to this chest was leaning against a poorly latched door during a winter storm. When he arrived the next morning, the wind had blown the door open and dumped the top into the snow where it sat for the night. Luckily it could be repaired. ∎

Reid says an improvement on the traditional frame-and-panel construction of this chest would be to make the legs from 12/4 material, eliminating the long seams between adjacent panels.

PANEL DETAIL

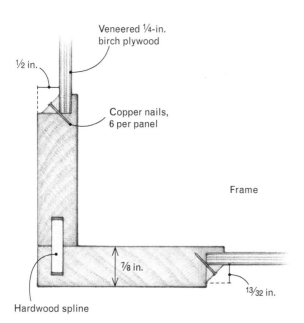

Veneered ¼-in. birch plywood

½ in.

Copper nails, 6 per panel

Frame

⅞ in.

13/32 in.

Hardwood spline

Danika's Chest

Details emerge in the making

TED BLACHLY
Warner, New Hampshire

DIMENSIONS
19 in. deep, 45 in. wide, 20 in. high

MATERIALS
Curly cherry, rosewood, leather (lid strap)

HARDWARE
Rosewood hinges, leather strap (lid)

FINISH
Varnish

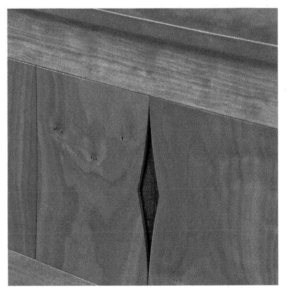

OPPOSITE Ted Blachly's cherry chest is evidence of his interest in both Danish and Japanese design. The concave ends are milled from solid wood.

TOP RIGHT Blachly formed the legs by cutting out a section at the bottom of the solid end and continuing the curved line of the leg into the field with carving tools. The tapered relief allows the leg to emerge gracefully from its surroundings.

BOTTOM RIGHT The only ornamentation on the chest is this rosewood diamond, a spline that connects the two adjacent panels.

Ted Blachly works mostly in solid material, so joinery that will accommodate the seasonal movement of wood is paramount to his designs. This chest was made for the first New Hampshire Furniture Masters auction in 1996 and still graces the home of that early patron, nothing in its construction showing any evidence of age.

Blachly had a free hand with the design, which grew out of sketches, drawings, and a lot of thought. By the time he got started, he had the shape and joinery mostly worked out and a full-scale shop drawing to guide him. But some of the key details, including the grip on the bottom edge of the lid and the legs, took their final shape as he built it.

"My drawing is not that great," he says. "I don't articulate all the details, shaping in particular, on paper. The piece usually comes out a lot better than I can draw it."

A key element of this chest is the solid ends, gently curved inward, slightly thicker at the top, and shaped at the bottom to form legs. To make the pieces, Blachly drew on a technique explained by Tage Frid in an early *Fine Woodworking* article. A router rides on a sled that is guided by a matched pair of curved rails running the length of the blank. Starting with material 2 in. thick, Blachly went back and forth over the surface with the router, the sled following the curve of the rails and gradually milling the end to its concave shape. "It's kind of like mowing a lawn," he says.

With the end blanks cut to shape, he formed the legs by cutting out a section of the bottom on a bandsaw. He continued the curved line of the leg into the panel and carved the tapered relief with carving tools.

The diamond-shaped panel at the center of the chest is a rosewood spline, ¼ in. thick, that is let into the edges of the two adjoining panels. Although the splines aren't visible elsewhere, they actually are located between each of the ¾-in.-thick panels on the front and back of the chest.

Rosewood also was Blachly's choice for the hinges. Their long leaves double as battens and help to keep the wide top from cupping. The hinges were among the most difficult parts of the chest

(CONTINUED)

to make and required full-scale drawings along with a mockup. The exercise prompted Blachly to strengthen the hinge knuckle when he moved on to the real thing.

Blachly, who has been making furniture since 1972, started his career with designs based on early New England furniture. He says he was later drawn to the work of Danish and Japanese artisans. All of those influences seem apparent here.

And the name, *Danika's Chest*? Blachly chose it to commemorate the birth of a friend's daughter. The chest now commands one end of a sunny living room, looking no less contemporary than the modern oil painting hanging on the wall behind it. Inside is a collection of tablecloths. ▪

ABOVE A mockup convinced Blachly to strengthen the knuckle of the rosewood hinges. The pieces pivot on a brass pin.

RIGHT The hinges are made from rosewood and double as battens that help keep the top of the chest flat.

Danika's Chest

This chest in solid cherry is designed to accommodate the seasonal expansion and contraction of the wood. Panels at the center of the front maintain the shape of the diamond while allowing the panels to move seasonallly.

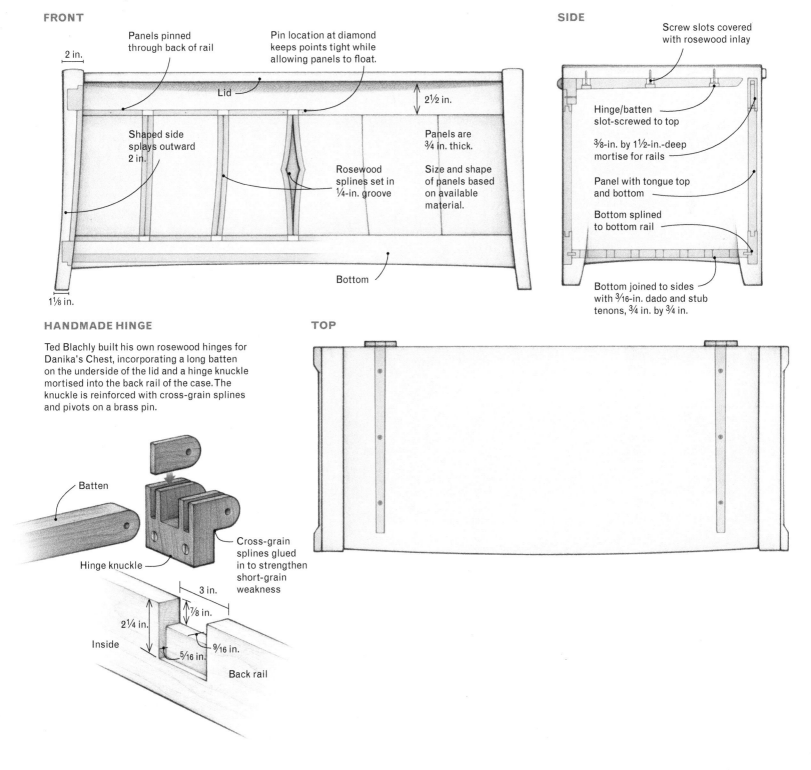

FRONT

Panels pinned through back of rail

Pin location at diamond keeps points tight while allowing panels to float.

2 in.

Lid

2½ in.

Shaped side splays outward 2 in.

Rosewood splines set in ¼-in. groove

Panels are ¾ in. thick.

Size and shape of panels based on available material.

1⅛ in.

Bottom

SIDE

Screw slots covered with rosewood inlay

Hinge/batten slot-screwed to top

⅜-in. by 1½-in.-deep mortise for rails

Panel with tongue top and bottom

Bottom splined to bottom rail

Bottom joined to sides with ³⁄₁₆-in. dado and stub tenons, ¾ in. by ¾ in.

HANDMADE HINGE

Ted Blachly built his own rosewood hinges for Danika's Chest, incorporating a long batten on the underside of the lid and a hinge knuckle mortised into the back rail of the case. The knuckle is reinforced with cross-grain splines and pivots on a brass pin.

Batten

Hinge knuckle

Cross-grain splines glued in to strengthen short-grain weakness

3 in.

⅞ in.

2¼ in.

Inside

⁵⁄₁₆ in.

⁹⁄₁₆ in.

Back rail

TOP

Chest in the Round

Ramping up a jewelry box design

GREGORY SMITH
Fort Bragg, California

DIMENSIONS	MATERIALS	HARDWARE	FINISH
22 in. deep, 34 in. wide, 19 in. tall	Teak, afzelia	Copper handle, brass hinges and lid stay	Oil/varnish outside, shellac and wax inside

Ordinarily, Gregory Smith would not choose a design for a spec piece that repeated something he'd already done. But he made an exception here, using a 15½-in.-long jewelry box he'd built previously as a design prototype for a chest twice its size.

It wasn't only the shape that drove the design, but also an exceptional piece of teak that Smith had tucked away. "Making a box this shape was itself an enjoyable challenge," Smith says, "but it was the piece of teak, with all its streaks and curls and personality, that kept me charged up through the whole process. It's a special piece of wood, and I tried to show it off as best I could."

Smith calls it a blanket chest because it's about the size a blanket chest ought to be and it certainly could hold four or five blankets. But he thinks it just as likely the chest could become a coffee table, with absolutely nothing stored inside.

To stretch the lumber as far as possible, Smith cut the plank into veneers and glued them to cores of four layers of ⅛-in. bending ply. The pieces were bent over a full-size form that mirrored the shape of the finished case and glued in a vacuum press. Because the chest is slightly oval, not a true round, each piece had to be formed on a specific part of the form.

The strong, light, and dimensionally stable panels could be doweled and glued to the bent-laminated end frames. The inside of the chest is finished in veneers of afzelia, an African hardwood.

The end frames, which make nearly a complete oval, were the most technically challenging part of the project, Smith says. He wasn't sure in the beginning he could get the laminations to take such sharp bends, especially given the reputation that oily teak has for making weak glue joints.

Smith, a graduate of the woodworking program at the College of the Redwoods, is exceptionally careful in developing designs. Once he's settled on a rough idea of what he wants to make, Smith settles in with a sketch pad to work out proportions and details and eventually a design emerges. "I usually know when this happens because I start drawing the same thing over and over," he says.

What follows is a full-scale mockup that allows Smith to see what the piece will look like at "full volume" and make any adjustments and changes that seem necessary.

(CONTINUED)

OPPOSITE Greg Smith's teak chest is based on a similar but much smaller jewelry box. Its curved panels were made in a vacuum press over a form shaped exactly like the finished chest.

ABOVE The handle is made from a piece of copper pipe that's been slightly squashed into an oval shape and filled with a wood dowel. The backplate for the handle also is a piece of copper pipe that has been flattened, textured, and let into the surface of the lid.

"I feel this part is extremely important," he says, "as this project will likely take considerable time and money and I want to be as sure as possible that the outcome will be good. There is nothing more demoralizing than trying to finish a piece that you have come to dislike."

Even so, there is still room to work in some changes as he goes along, details that he could not have anticipated at the start. "Often these things are my favorites," he says. ■

To make the lid, Smith formed the plywood core first, then added edge-banding to the ends. The top and bottom veneers came next, effectively capturing the solid-wood edging.

Chest in the Round

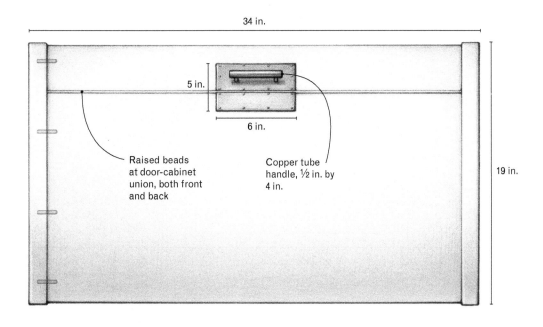

34 in.

5 in.

6 in.

19 in.

Raised beads at door-cabinet union, both front and back

Copper tube handle, ½ in. by 4 in.

Chest Made in Sections

Smith divided the ovoid chest into quadrants and made each section separately over a full-size form in a vacuum press. Chest components were made from four plies of bending plywood and veneer.

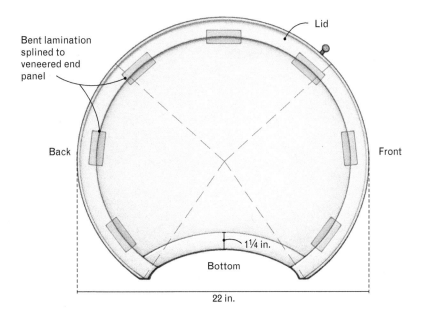

Bent lamination splined to veneered end panel

Lid

Back

Front

1¼ in.

Bottom

22 in.

Curly Cherry Classic

Clean lines and lots of dovetails

CHARLES DURFEE
Woolwich, Maine

DIMENSIONS	MATERIALS	HARDWARE	FINISH
20 in. deep, 40½ in. wide, 27 in. high	Pennsylvania curly cherry, pine, poplar, cedar	Brass butt hinges, brass chain lid stay	Minwax Antique Oil

OPPOSITE Charles Durfee's curly cherry chest has its roots in Shaker design. Simple lines, sound proportions, and highly figured wood give it enduring appeal.

BELOW Dovetails unify the design, as well as keep things together. Hidden dovetail cleats allow cross-grain construction without the risk of problems caused by seasonal movement.

It won't come as much of a surprise to learn that Shaker and Colonial styles have been important design influences for Maine furniture maker Charles Durfee. Although not an exact reproduction, this chest in Pennsylvania curly cherry has all the characteristics of a quintessential 19th-century Shaker blanket box.

Durfee describes it as something of a transition piece, functionally falling between a simple six-board chest and a more elaborate chests of drawers. Its single drawer makes the interior space more accessible, and therefore more useful, but the case fundamentally is still a box with a lid.

It is with simple forms like these that Shaker craftsmen exerted such a profound influence on many furniture makers who would follow. Their religious beliefs helped guide them toward an unadorned, spare style, but their exacting craftsmanship and careful proportions held wide appeal, and their deceptively simple approach to furniture is still popular.

Durfee chose some outstanding curly cherry to make the chest, lowering the height of the case by an inch so he could use a single board across the front. Shakers would have been likely to stain or paint a piece like this, Durfee says, but a rubbed oil finish brings out the natural glow of the wood. Inside the box is a cedar lining to keep blankets smelling fresh.

One thing that doesn't change is the construction techniques that allow wood to move seasonally. In this case, trim pieces on the lower front edges of the case are attached with dovetail cleats, as are the side moldings on the lid. This allows wide pieces to expand and shrink across their width with changes in humidity while trim pieces remain the same length.

Dovetails that join the case sides, as well as the drawer front, are a prominent feature of Shaker casework. Durfee no doubt has cut thousands of them during his 30-plus years as a furniture maker, but he admits that accurately cutting and assembling long rows of dovetails still has its moments.

And he's still learning. After three decades in the business, Durfee realizes "that a piece of furniture can often take on a life of its own. This chest has been one of those for me." ▪

Curly Cherry Classic

This dovetailed chest by Charles Durfee incorporates many visual and structural elements of Shaker furniture. The side molding on the lid and the trim pieces on the sides of the drawer opening are mounted with dovetailed keys, which allow for seasonal wood movement.

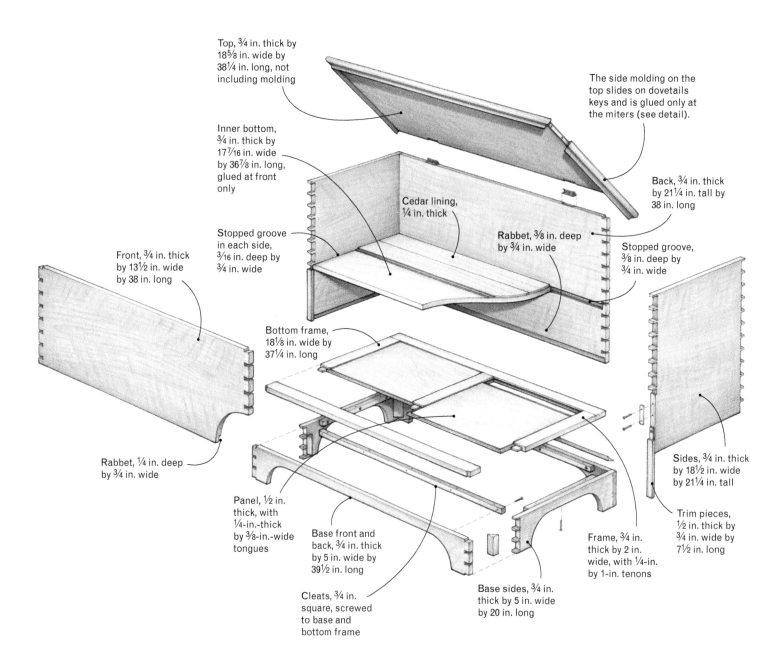

Top, ¾ in. thick by 18⅝ in. wide by 38¼ in. long, not including molding

The side molding on the top slides on dovetails keys and is glued only at the miters (see detail).

Inner bottom, ¾ in. thick by 17⁷⁄₁₆ in. wide by 36⅞ in. long, glued at front only

Cedar lining, ¼ in. thick

Back, ¾ in. thick by 21¼ in. tall by 38 in. long

Stopped groove in each side, ³⁄₁₆ in. deep by ¾ in. wide

Rabbet, ⅜ in. deep by ¾ in. wide

Stopped groove, ⅜ in. deep by ¾ in. wide

Front, ¾ in. thick by 13½ in. wide by 38 in. long

Bottom frame, 18⅛ in. wide by 37¼ in. long

Rabbet, ¼ in. deep by ¾ in. wide

Sides, ¾ in. thick by 18½ in. wide by 21¼ in. tall

Panel, ½ in. thick, with ¼-in.-thick by ⅜-in.-wide tongues

Base front and back, ¾ in. thick by 5 in. wide by 39½ in. long

Frame, ¾ in. thick by 2 in. wide, with ¼-in. by 1-in. tenons

Trim pieces, ½ in. thick by ¾ in. wide by 7½ in. long

Cleats, ¾ in. square, screwed to base and bottom frame

Base sides, ¾ in. thick by 5 in. wide by 20 in. long

40½ in.

13½ in.

27 in.

39½ in.

20 in.

21¼ in.

5 in.

19¾ in.

Top Molding Detail

The molding consists of a half-round and a cove glued together and attached to the chest lid.

Lipped Front Drawer

The cherry drawer front is lipped on the top and sides. The sides, back, and bottom of the drawer are made of a secondary wood.

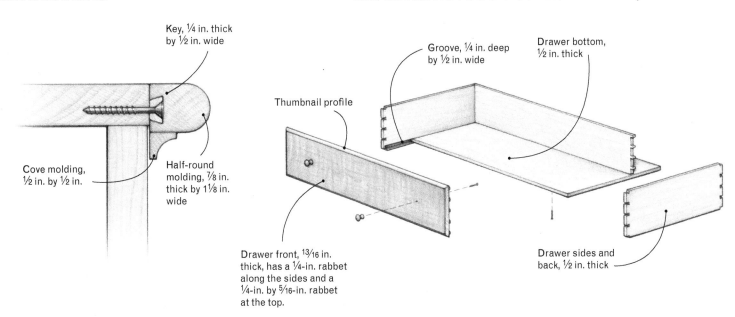

Key, ¼ in. thick by ½ in. wide

Cove molding, ½ in. by ½ in.

Half-round molding, ⅞ in. thick by 1⅛ in. wide

Groove, ¼ in. deep by ½ in. wide

Drawer bottom, ½ in. thick

Thumbnail profile

Drawer front, ¹³/₁₆ in. thick, has a ¼-in. rabbet along the sides and a ¼-in. by ⁵/₁₆-in. rabbet at the top.

Drawer sides and back, ½ in. thick

Celebrating Arts and Crafts

One style that never seems to fade

DARRELL PEART
Seattle, Washington

DIMENSIONS	MATERIALS	HARDWARE	FINISH
22½ in. deep, 45⅛ in. wide, 16¹³/₁₆ in. high	African mahogany, ebony	Torsion lid supports	General Finishes dye stain (orange and medium brown), General Finishes Armor-R-Seal Satin

TOP RIGHT The Greene brothers often used a decorative ebony spline to join a breadboard end to a panel, as Peart does here.

BOTTOM RIGHT Peart made faux strapping at the base of this chest from wood. The only known example of this motif in the work of Greene and Greene is in a letter box for a house in Pasadena, California. Although a photograph exists, the box itself has disappeared.

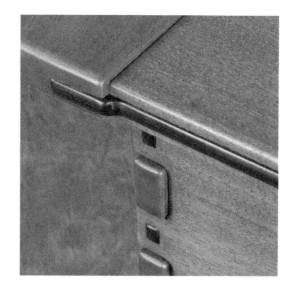

Anyone who has been lucky enough to tour the Gamble House in Pasadena, California, will instantly recognize the unmistakable design antecedents of this chest by Darrell Peart in African mahogany and ebony.

The interlocking finger joints, ebony plugs and decorative splines, and offset breadboard ends all are hallmarks of designs by brothers Charles and Henry Greene. Their work in the early 20th century on famously upscale bungalows like the Gamble House, as well as interior furniture and fittings, defined the high-water mark of the Arts and Crafts movement in the United States.

Although the basic design elements of this chest are clearly from the Greene and Greene repertoire, blanket chests themselves were not. Peart knows of one Greene and Greene blanket chest, at a house built for Charles Millard Pratt in Ojai, California, between 1908 and 1911. The chest shares some similarities with this one, but also many differences.

In addition to imparting his own style to this chest, Peart had some tinkering to do with this piece before he thought the proportions were correct. He started with an overall plan in his head and began drawing the chest to settle its proportions as well as the placement of the shaped wooden straps at the base. He found the base on his first draft too big, and it took a couple of other tries before it looked right.

"Probably the thing I am most conscious of was the need to go lighter on the base," he says, meaning not as much height. "Typically I design and build pieces that are at least 30 in. high. On a low-profile piece such as this, the base needs to be toned down just a bit."

The distinctive strapping at the base of the chest apparently has few precedents in Greene and Greene designs, although the general motif seems familiar. Peart says he knows of one instance of this, on a letter case made for the living room in the Freeman A. Ford house in Pasadena, although there they were leather rather than wood (see the sidebar on p. 110).

Much of Peart's work is in the Greene and Greene style, although he does accurate reproductions only occasionally. His work is mostly interpretative, using many Greene and Greene details without duplicating a piece in its entirety. (Peart's book *Greene & Greene: Design Elements for the Workshop* was published by Linden in 2006.)

OPPOSITE Blanket chests are a rarity in the work of Greene and Greene, but the interlocking finger joints at the corners of this chest by Darrell Peart are one signature detail of these Arts and Crafts giants.

(CONTINUED)

MYSTERY CHEST

Darrell Peart's blanket chest includes wooden pieces at the base shaped to look like reinforcing straps (see the sidebar on pp. 112-113 for how he made them). Many of the stylistic details in Peart's work are derived from the work of Charles and Henry Greene, but the strapping was an uncommon touch for these icons of the Arts and Crafts age. The one known example comes from a letter case in a Greene and Greene house in Pasadena, California, built for Freeman A. Ford, vice president of the Pasadena Ice Co., in 1906.

Peart first saw a photo of the case in Randell Makinson's book, *Greene & Greene: Furniture and Related Designs.* He made a number of fruitless inquiries before calling Makinson and learning that the photo was in his files.

The letter box itself, however, has vanished. Peart contacted descendants of the Ford family and tracked down other leads without finding it. One story has it that many pieces from the Ford house are in a storage unit somewhere in the California desert. "Too vague and no way to trace," Peart says.

One positive outcome, though: Thanks to Peart's efforts, the photo ended up in the Greene and Greene archives where a larger public will be able to enjoy it.

Peart also draws on work by James Krenov, whose books on woodworking were among the few resources available when he first took up the craft.

The Greene brothers had several recipes for finish, including one that included potassium dichromate and linseed oil. The potassium compound gives wood a rich, brown color. But Peart says he was dissuaded from using it because of its health risks. He looked for a substitute that replicates the feel of the original without the hazards.

He settled on a wipe-on/wipe-off finish made by General Finishes, which passed rigorous durability tests before Peart started using it. A client had asked for a dependable finish because he had dogs that had a habit of drooling all over the furniture. Peart made up some samples with different finishes and sent them off. The dogs did their best, but the finish survived. ∎

Celebrating Arts and Crafts

Darrell Peart's chest is made from African mahogany, joined at the corners with oversize finger joints, a hallmark of Greene and Greene designs of the Arts and Crafts era. Details are in ebony.

TOP

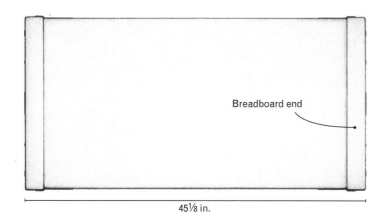

Breadboard end

45⅛ in.

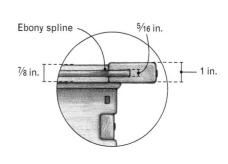

Ebony spline

⁵⁄₁₆ in.

⅞ in.

1 in.

FRONT

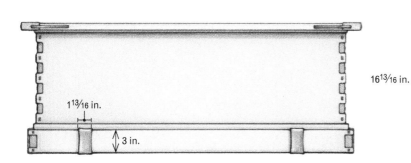

1¹³⁄₁₆ in.

3 in.

SIDE

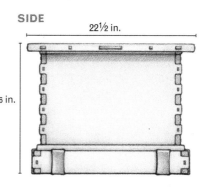

22½ in.

16¹³⁄₁₆ in.

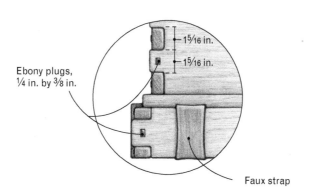

Ebony plugs,
¼ in. by ⅜ in.

1⁵⁄₁₆ in.

1⁵⁄₁₆ in.

Faux strap

MAKING FAUX STRAPS FOR THE CHEST BASE

Arts and Crafts designers Charles and Henry Greene incorporated leather straps in the base molding of a letter case designed for the Freeman Ford house in Pasadena, California. It is the only known example of this detail in their work.

Darrell Peart works in the Greene and Greene style, and he liked the detail enough to include it in a blanket chest he made. But instead of leather, he made the faux straps from wood. Here are his instructions.

Start by preparing and milling stock $^{15}/_{16}$ in. by $2^{1}/_{32}$ in. by 30 in. long. With the tablesaw blade set at a height of $^{3}/_{16}$ in., mill a cove down the center of the stock using a fence set 45 degrees to the blade. Cut the stock into pieces $3^{5}/_{16}$ in. long (you'll need eight of them).

Using a shopmade template, rout a 3-in. radius across the top of the pieces with a flush trim bit *(photo 1)*.

With a $^{3}/_{16}$-in. radius core box bit (that's $^{3}/_{8}$ in. dia.), rout to a depth of $^{9}/_{16}$ in. and $^{5}/_{16}$ in. back from the longest point of the front edge *(photo 2)*. Make the cut in three passes using push cauls of different heights. The $^{3}/_{16}$-in. radius will mate with the $^{3}/_{16}$-in. radius on the top edge of the base.

1. Peart starts a strap by cutting a radius in one end on a shaper.

2. Using a core box bit, cut a profile at the top of the block in three passes.

With a shopmade template and flush-trim bit, rout a 30-in. radius down both sides of the stock *(photo 3)*. Then bandsaw the backside of the face to meet the prerouted radius corner *(photo 4)*.

Sand the coved face and top profile with a spindle sander and a 4-in. sleeve. Slightly round over the corner joining the front and top faces *(photo 5)*.

Stretch some sticky-backed 80-grit sandpaper over a piece of stock that has a 1/8-in. radius on the top corner. Use this to sand smooth and shape and fit the back side that wraps around the base. (The 1/8-in. radius with sandpaper over it comes close to the 3/16-in. radius on the base.) Starting with 80-grit paper, smooth over all the sharp edges on the outside face.

Trim the lip by first cutting on the bandsaw to within 1/16 in. oversize. Put a strip of sticky-backed 80-grit paper on the edge of the case bottom just above the base at the exact location of the individual strap. Position the strap on the base with paper equal to the thickness of the 80-grit sandpaper between the face of the base and inside face of the strap. Slide the strap back and forth so that the leading edge of the lip contacts the sandpaper. Continue until the sandpaper ceases to remove material. Remove the sandpaper for a perfect fit. Finally, glue the strap in place.

3. Add a gentle radius to the sides of the block with a flush-trim bit.

5. A spindle sander smooths the face and edges of the strap.

4. Cut away the back of the block on a bandsaw.

Alabama Man

Combining seating and storage

J-P VILKMAN
Helsinki, Finland

DIMENSIONS	MATERIALS	HARDWARE	FINISH
17¾ in. deep, 59 in. wide, 23⅝ in. high	Mahogany, ebony, white oak	Brass butt hinges	Osmo® color oil wax

J-P Vilkman made this combination bench and storage case as a woodworking student in his native Finland, and now 10 years later he still finds the design well balanced even if he can't explain exactly how the piece earned its name.

"I wanted to create a piece that could be used in different places in your house," Vilkman says. "If you don't have too much room, you want to use the space well. This piece combines two functions in one, which makes it handy."

Vilkman built the piece from a single plank of mahogany. The posts are solid wood. Panels are sawn veneer over lumbercore plywood and joined to the rails with splines.

The wedged through tenons are a common detail in Art Nouveau and Arts and Crafts furniture, Vilkman says, whereas the ebony wedges are a clear reference to the work of Greene and Greene.

"I chose veneered panels over solid wood because that way I could control the grain and color better," Vilkman says, "and I didn't have to worry about wood movement, which is a big problem in Finland."

Vilkman is one of those furniture makers who firmly believes in building mockups to test designs that originate on paper. It is the only way, he says, to know how the finished piece will look and feel. He uses whatever he has on hand—"cheap solid wood" such as poplar or pine, medium-density fiberboard, cardboard, and hot-melt glue.

The overall proportions and shape of the legs were key issues for this piece, but even a mockup couldn't settle every detail. Vilkman waited to shape the handrails until the rest of the bench had been assembled. That way, he could see how all of it fit together.

Vilkman has been making furniture for 20 years, but he comes to the profession as a second career. His first was as an electrical technician who repaired and maintained electronic equipment in hospitals. He quit that in 1989 and went to school to learn woodworking, then went on to learn how to build wooden boats. Later, he came across an article about College of the Redwoods in California and decided to apply. His two years there studying under James Krenov were pivotal.

Vilkman continues to move forward with his work. "I used to like a lot of the Art Deco period," he says, "but right now my work is changing. I am heading toward more sculptural work. I think what I'm doing right now is minimalistic functional sculpture."

OPPOSITE This chest is intended to double as a bench in a house where there's not a lot of room to spare. Cutting solid parts and veneer from a single board helps minimize variations in grain and color, and using veneered panels helps control unwanted wood movement.

ABOVE RIGHT Through tenons detailed with ebony wedges are a reference to the work of Arts and Crafts designers Greene and Greene.

ABOVE LEFT The ebony handle on the lid contrasts nicely with the mahogany, another Greene and Greene detail.

Alabama Man

J-P Vilkman's chest is a mix of solid lumber and veneered panels, all cut from a single plank of mahogany. The interior storage tray is made from white oak.

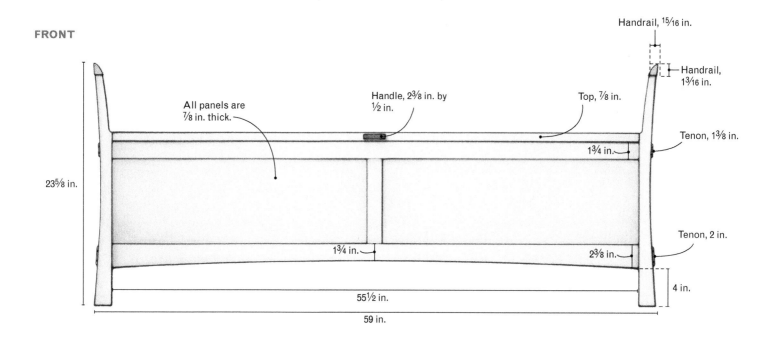

Handrail, 15/16 in.

Handrail, 13/16 in.

All panels are 7/8 in. thick.

Handle, 2 3/8 in. by 1/2 in.

Top, 7/8 in.

Tenon, 1 3/8 in.

1 3/4 in.

23 5/8 in.

Tenon, 2 in.

1 3/4 in.

2 3/8 in.

4 in.

55 1/2 in.

59 in.

TOP

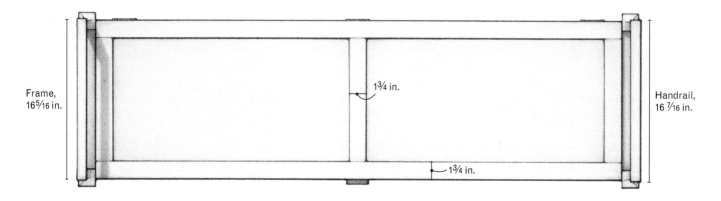

Frame, 16 5/16 in.

1 3/4 in.

Handrail, 16 7/16 in.

1 3/4 in.

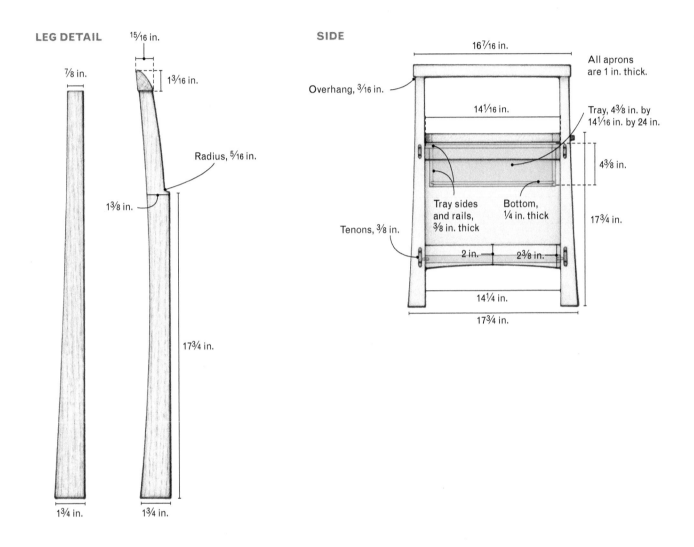

LEG DETAIL

7/8 in.

15/16 in.

1 3/16 in.

Radius, 5/16 in.

1 3/8 in.

17 3/4 in.

1 3/4 in.

1 3/4 in.

SIDE

16 7/16 in.

All aprons
are 1 in. thick.

Overhang, 3/16 in.

14 1/16 in.

Tray, 4 3/8 in. by
14 1/16 in. by 24 in.

4 3/8 in.

Tray sides
and rails,
3/8 in. thick

Bottom,
1/4 in. thick

17 3/4 in.

Tenons, 3/8 in.

2 in.

2 3/8 in.

14 1/4 in.

17 3/4 in.

A Wedding Chest

Borrowing a Moorish motif

MIGUEL GÓMEZ-IBÁÑEZ
Boston, Massachusetts

DIMENSIONS	MATERIALS	HARDWARE	FINISH
16⅞ in. deep, 44 in. wide, 22½ in. high	Peruvian walnut, purpleheart, ebony, German silver	Custom-forged wrought-iron hinges	Oil/urethane

Miguel Gómez-Ibáñez is not only an accomplished woodworker but also the president of the North Bennet Street School in Boston's North End, home to one of the country's best known furniture-making programs. So it's no small feat that he found the time and patience to build a chest incorporating nearly 500 pieces of inch-long molding.

Yet the applied molding is key to the design, second in a series of five wedding chests he plans to build for his four children and a godchild (the first of them appeared in Taunton's *Design Book 8* in 2009). The geometric pattern, reflecting Gómez-Ibáñez's interest in Islamic art, is derived from the intricate coffered ceilings common in Spanish churches.

Because his designs are worked out precisely before he begins work, Gómez-Ibáñez labored over the details. And the first decision was a structural one: how to build the carcase. A frame-and-panel surface pattern would have been true to the design's 13th-century Moorish heritage, but ultimately he decided it wasn't feasible. Instead, he settled on a dovetailed case of solid wood, then removed material in the field and framed the recesses with molding. It looks a lot like a frame-and-panel assembly but it isn't.

Each of the recesses is about ½ in. deep. The tiny pieces of molding, which he made on a router table, are L-shaped so they hide the edge of the recess and lap over the top edge slightly into the field. There is some chance that the joints between some molding pieces could open up over time due to this cross-grain construction, but the longest pieces perpendicular to the grain, on the lower reaches of the chest, are only about 7 in. long, minimizing the risk.

To help the paneled areas stand out in the field of Peruvian walnut, Gómez-Ibáñez veneered the bottom of each recess with purpleheart, pressing the veneer in place with a specially made caul.

Cutting and fitting the 492 pieces of molding was challenging enough, but finishing them also added a layer of complexity. Gómez-Ibáñez doesn't use spray equipment, so each of the many surfaces had to be tackled by hand.

The wrought-iron hardware is custom formed. A silver medallion on the front of the case will have details of the wedding engraved in its surface when that time comes.

The chest series is a way for Gómez-Ibáñez to keep his hand in woodworking while heading North Bennet Street, where he can't accept regular commissions. All of the chests, he says, will be different but equally complex. ▪

OPPOSITE One of a series of five, Miguel Gómez-Ibáñez's Peruvian walnut chest was made as a wedding gift for one of his children. The pattern of the applied molding is derived from a Moorish design common to Spanish churches.

Gómez-Ibáñez combined three different woods in the complex detailing for this chest: a field of Peruvian walnut, recesses veneered with purpleheart, and small squares of ebony.

A silver medallion on the front of the chest will eventually be engraved with the name of one of Gómez-Ibáñez's children.

A Wedding Chest

This walnut wedding chest by Miguel Gómez-Ibáñez recreates a Moorish decorative motif with excavated areas in the field trimmed with hundreds of tiny pieces of molding.

FRONT

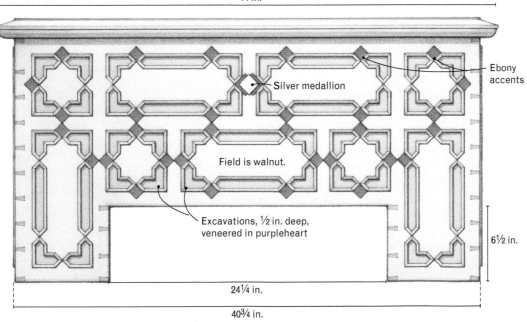

44 in.

Silver medallion

Ebony accents

Field is walnut.

Excavations, ½ in. deep, veneered in purpleheart

6½ in.

24¼ in.

40¾ in.

SIDE

16⅞ in.

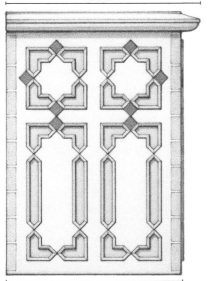

22½ in.

15¼ in.

Cabinetmaking Traditions

A knock-out piece of lumber, rock solid joinery

BRUCE EATON

Hampton, New Hampshire

DIMENSIONS	MATERIALS	HARDWARE	FINISH
18 in. deep, 35 in. wide, 21 in. high	Spalted curly soft maple, aromatic cedar	Traditional butt hinges, piston-type lid stay	Oil/varnish

ruce Eaton, a civil and environmental engineer before he became a furniture maker, was a student at Boston's North Bennet Street School when he landed the commission for this chest. It was an unusually fine piece of curly maple that helped make it special.

The chest was ordered by a woman who, logically enough, wanted a piece of furniture at the end of her bed for storing blankets. For Eaton, it became an exercise in cabinetmaking, a chance to use a number of classic construction techniques that he'd been learning about in school. There are the mitered and splined front corners of the case, the half-blind dovetails for the back of the case, mitered ogee bracket feet, and mortise-and-tenon joinery for the frames.

Eaton, who shares a shop with four others in an old New Hampshire textile mill, worked from full-scale drawings but didn't need a prototype for this traditionally styled case. What helped was finding a flitch of curly spalted maple at an estate sale in Northwood, New Hampshire. An amateur sawyer had apparently found the tree by the side of a road and with help from his son hauled it home and cut it into planks. When he died unexpectedly, the lumber had to be sold to settle his estate.

Although the circumstances of the sale were sad, Eaton was delighted to find the small flitch. He assumed it had been passed over by many other potential buyers because of its short length and because the wood had started to spalt. But it was just the right amount for his design.

"I really loved the lumber I found for the chest," Eaton says. "The photos don't really do it justice. It was 20-plus inches wide with tight curl throughout. The colors were also really pretty, especially raw before finish was applied."

The bracket feet, overhanging lid, and simple moldings certainly give the chest a period look. Eaton says it's not based on any specific examples, although he saw similar chests under construction while a student at North Bennet Street and also came across one like it in Thomas Chippendale's 1762 *The Gentleman's & Cabinet-Maker's Director.*

He modified his original drawings to better fit the lumber, and also played with the dimensions of the ogee feet before he was satisfied with their proportions. He made them slightly wider than they might have been in a strict Chippendale reproduction because they looked too narrow in his drawings.

(CONTINUED)

OPPOSITE Bruce Eaton's spalted curly maple chest clearly has its roots in early American design. Splined mitered corners at the front of the case do nothing to interrupt the dramatic figure of the wood.

ABOVE At the back of the case, a dovetailed panel joins the two sides. Just like joinery at the front of the case, there are no visible seams to mar the figure of the maple.

On a taller case, narrower feet might have looked appropriate, he adds, but on a more horizontal case like this one, the wider feet just looked better.

One advantage in Eaton's choice of joinery is that the grain of the wood flows seamlessly around the case. Neither the miter at the front of the case nor the half-blind dovetails at the back offer any interference visually.

The lid is supported by a piston-type slide when it opens. Inside the case, Eaton installed a shiplapped bottom of cedar boards. ▪

Cabinetmaking Traditions

Bruce Eaton's classic chest incorporates splined miter joints at the front of the case and half-blind dovetails joining the back to the sides. The lid is attached to a subframe that helps to keep the top flat, its mitered corners reinforced with splines. (For a look at how Eaton made the splined miters for the case, see the sidebar on pp. 126–127.)

TOP

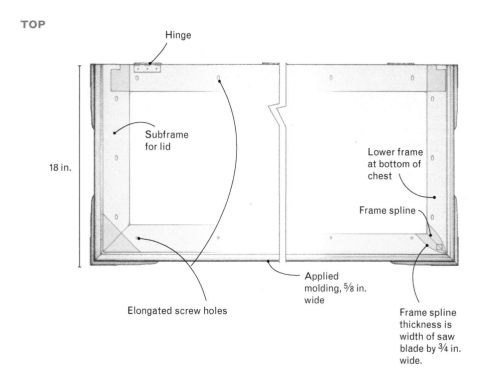

Hinge

Subframe for lid

Lower frame at bottom of chest

Frame spline

18 in.

Applied molding, ⅝ in. wide

Elongated screw holes

Frame spline thickness is width of saw blade by ¾ in. wide.

FRONT

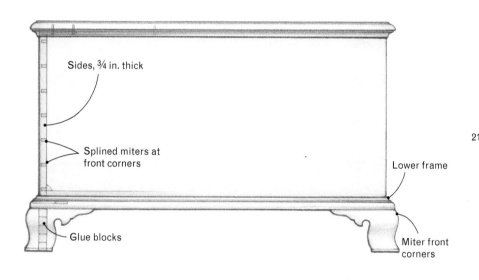

Sides, ¾ in. thick

Splined miters at front corners

Lower frame

Glue blocks

Miter front corners

SIDE

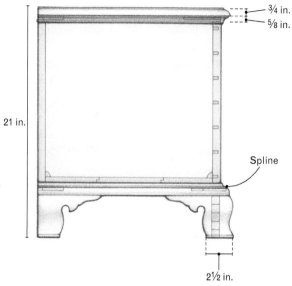

¾ in.

⅝ in.

21 in.

Spline

2½ in.

BACK

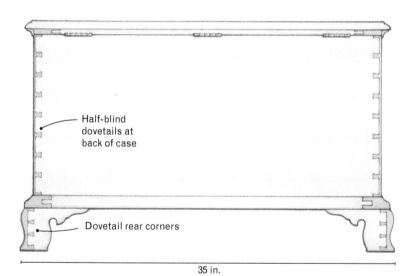

Half-blind dovetails at back of case

Dovetail rear corners

35 in.

MAKING BLIND KEYS FOR A MITER

The front corners of Bruce Eaton's blanket chest are joined with miters that have been reinforced with small keys of solid wood. Unlike biscuits or continuous splines of wood, the keys are inserted into the miter so they have a long-grain-to-long-grain gluing surface, the strongest kind of glued connection. Although the keys are small, they significantly strengthen the joint and lessen the possibility the miter will open up over time.

The process starts with the construction of a router template that's used to cut mortises in the face of two adjacent miters simultaneously. The mortises are stopped short of the top and bottom faces by about 3/16 in. so they won't be seen when the joint is assembled.

After laying out these parallel lines on the miters, butt the two pieces together and measure across the joint from one top line to the other *(photo 1)*. This distance represents the length of the slots that will be cut in the template to guide the router.

On a piece of 1/4-in. plywood or MDF, lay out a series of slots. Keep the ones on the end far enough from the edges of the workpiece to allow for any rabbets, profiles, or other edge treatments. Using a guide fence and stop blocks, mill the slots

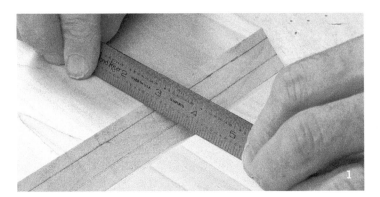

1. Measure across the joint and use this dimension to size the slots in the template.

2. Lay out a series of slots along a centerline on the template.

3. After all the slots have been cut in the template, insert the guide collar on the bottom of the router and switch bits.

4. Butt two mitered edges together, clamp the template over them, and mill the mortises in both pieces at the same time.

with a router bit the same size as the router's guide collar *(photo 2)*.

Once this series of slots is cut into the template, insert the guide collar in the router along with its companion bit, butt two adjoining mitered pieces together, and clamp the work securely *(photo 3)*. Make sure the edges of the two pieces are aligned precisely and that the template is centered over the joint. Set the depth of cut so the bit just strikes the bottom layout line, and rout the mortises in both pieces at the same time *(photo 4)*. You'll end up with opposing pairs of mortises in the mitered faces of the workpieces *(photo 5)*. The mortises should be squared up with a chisel *(photo 6)*.

Mill up some solid stock to fit the mortises, and chop them to length. The keys should just reach the layout lines on the mitered faces. Glue the keys into the face of one of the workpieces, tapping them snugly into place with a hammer *(photo 7)*.

Now bring the two workpieces together and check for alignment *(photo 8)*. Make adjustments, then glue and clamp the miter together. Working one step at a time, glue a corner, assemble the rest of the case dry, let the glue set, then move to the next corner.

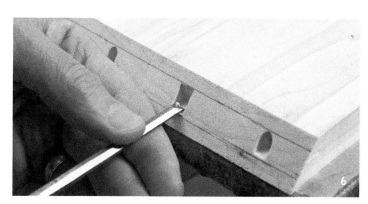

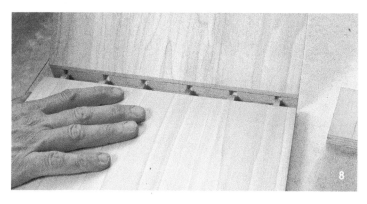

5. Mitered edges now have pairs of opposing mortises.

6. Square up the mortises with a chisel.

7. Glue in short keys of solid material. Tap them into place with a hammer.

8. Check for proper alignment before gluing.

Pilgrim Century

Not a reproduction but a look

DAVID STENSTROM
Portland, Maine

DIMENSIONS
20 in. deep, 46 in. wide,
34 in. high

MATERIALS
Rift-sawn red oak, figured
poplar, aromatic cedar

HARDWARE
Hand-forged hinges

FINISH
Oil, paint

David Stenstrom was looking for ideas from the "Pilgrim Century" when he came up with a design for this painted oak chest. He looked at a variety of examples in books he had on hand, eventually combining a number of design elements that he found appealing.

After 20 years, the design still works. It's loosely patterned after a Connecticut Sunflower chest, a style dating from the 17th century, which often featured a carved sunflower on the central panel. It also shows some resemblance to a Hadley chest, another early American design first discovered in a central Massachusetts town of the same name (for a modern interpretation of a Hadley chest, see Brian Reid's work on p. 92).

Wallace Nutting, the collector, author, and for a time furniture producer, was enamored with sunflower chests and even added one to his retail catalog of furniture reproductions. "It is beyond doubt," the listing said, "the greatest and noblest furniture heritage from the American past."

Stenstrom's chest is less elaborate than these early examples. As circumstances of the times would have dictated, it features three inset panels and two drawers on the front face and is constructed in a traditional style that favored strength, durability, and simplicity over furniture-making acrobatics. The case features mortise-and-tenon joinery, and the drawers were constructed with dovetails. The bottom of the chest, along with the back panels, is made from cedar.

Early sunflower chests were often jazzed up with carving and applied elements, such as turned half-columns, as well as paint. Stenstrom skipped the carving and chose a limited color palette to highlight the front of the chest. The figured red oak for the panels—not the easiest thing to get his hands on—provides plenty of impact.

The top of the chest is the same red and black, painted in a style called "tortoise shelling." It would not have been found on chests of the period but reflects Stenstrom's interest in decorative painting at the time. Stenstrom thought at the time that the red and black paints were probably a bold departure from the decorations on very early American pieces, but in hindsight he's not so sure. Bright colors weren't uncommon at the time, even though they've faded in the intervening years furthering the notion that furniture from that period was dull or drab.

(CONTINUED)

Pilgrim Century

David Stenstrom's chest is a simplified version of an early American style, without the intricate carving that might have characterized the original but the same sturdy construction. The back panels of the chest and drawers are one-piece cedar, and the case is assembled with mortise-and-tenon joints.

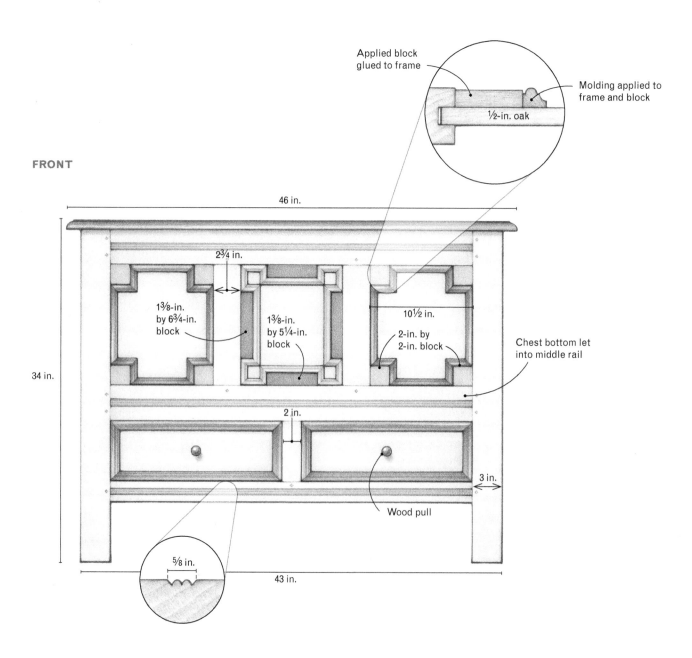

Applied block glued to frame

Molding applied to frame and block

½-in. oak

FRONT

46 in.

2¾ in.

1⅜-in. by 6¾-in. block

1⅜-in. by 5¼-in. block

10½ in.

2-in. by 2-in. block

Chest bottom let into middle rail

34 in.

2 in.

3 in.

Wood pull

⅝ in.

43 in.

"I wanted to make something in the form of the old chests," Stenstrom says, "but I wanted it to be fun or less serious than the old ones. Life was hard in America in the Pilgrim Century. However, as I look at pictures of the old chests, maybe they were fun, too, and it's just the old black-and-white photos that make them look somber." ∎

DRAWER DETAIL

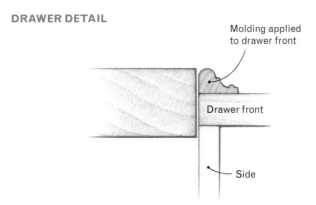

Molding applied to drawer front

Drawer front

Side

SIDE

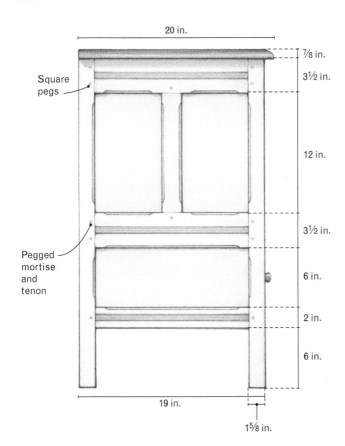

20 in.

Square pegs

Pegged mortise and tenon

⅞ in.

3½ in.

12 in.

3½ in.

6 in.

2 in.

6 in.

19 in.

1⅝ in.

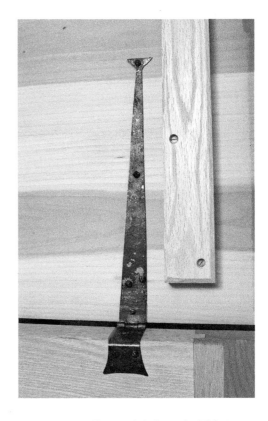

Battens help keep the lid flat. The inside of the chest has been left unfinished. The hand-forged hinges are from Ball & Ball.

Function Meets Elegance

Bleached white ash makes clean, contemporary storage

SHONA KINNIBURGH
Glasgow, Scotland

DIMENSIONS	MATERIALS	HARDWARE	FINISH
16 in. deep, 39 in. wide, 18 in. high	Ash, poplar	Satin nickel butt hinges	Bleaching agent, wax

Shona Kinniburgh was part of the nine-month program at the Center for Furniture Craftsmanship in Rockport, Maine—what she calls a "life-changing decision"—when she made this chest as a class assignment. It was the first piece of furniture that she designed as well as built, and she got plenty of feedback from her mates as well as her instructors, David Upfill-Brown and Brian Reid. They weren't sure about the proportions of the deep bottom drawers and relatively shallow top tray, but Kinniburgh stood her ground. What she had in mind was a chest for a hall, not a bedroom, where hats, gloves, and scarves could be kept. It needed copious amounts of accessible storage, and it had to be sturdy enough to be used as a bench.

The chest actually began its incubation as a floor-standing cabinet, which would have fulfilled terms of the class assignment. She was looking for something "shapely and slightly curvaceous," but when the project got past sketches to the point of building a mockup, Kinniburgh discovered she didn't like what it looked like.

"It was literally back to the drawing board," she says, "and the idea for something more useful evolved, blending function, practicality, and a touch of elegance. The idea crystallized into the current chest. Although I lost time at the design stage, it saved me from wasting material, time, and effort by finding out after I had started that it wasn't going to work."

The case is made from white ash, a durable hardwood but not Kinniburgh's first choice. She wasn't wild about its open grain or its tendency to darken and yellow over time. But with encouragement to try a bleached finish, Kinniburgh decided to give it a shot and was delighted with the results.

Although Kinniburgh had originally intended to do all of the joinery by hand, she subsequently discovered the Festool Domino, a jazzed-up biscuit joiner that cuts mortises for matching slip tenons. Those are used to join the base and middle shelves to the two massive ends. Front and back rails are joined to the ends with floating tenons. The drawer dovetails were cut by hand.

Kinniburgh shaped the end pieces on a bandsaw before they were glued up, and finished them with a plane (used across the grain) and a card scraper. The two-part bleaching finish was a little finicky to apply, but achieved the effect she was looking for.

OPPOSITE Shona Kinniburgh's hall chest was designed to provide lots of accessible storage for hats, gloves, and scarves in two drawers as well as a compartment under the lid. The 1-in.-thick top also makes a comfortable place to sit while putting on or taking off shoes and boots.

ABOVE Kinniburgh especially likes the tactile quality in the grain of the chest ends.

(CONTINUED)

Function Meets Elegance

Shona Kinniburgh's hall chest includes two deep storage drawers and a relatively shallow compartment above them. The interior partition and base are joined to the ends with Festool Dominos; drawer dovetails were cut by hand. The ends of the case are 2½ in. thick at the top and taper toward the floor.

TOP

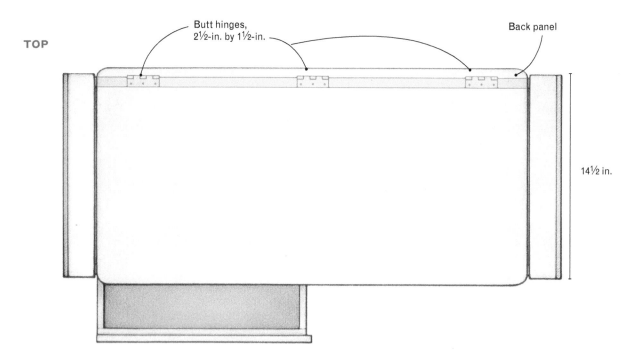

Butt hinges,
2½-in. by 1½-in.

Back panel

14½ in.

FRONT

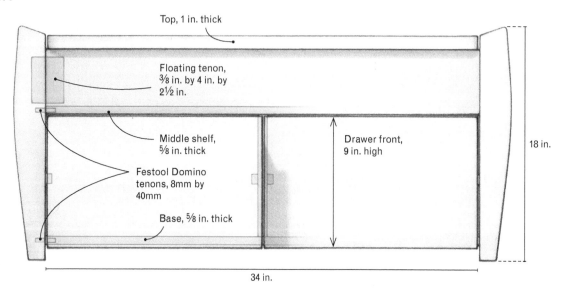

Top, 1 in. thick

Floating tenon,
⅜ in. by 4 in. by
2½ in.

Middle shelf,
⅝ in. thick

Festool Domino
tenons, 8mm by
40mm

Base, ⅝ in. thick

Drawer front,
9 in. high

18 in.

34 in.

After the program ended, Kinniburgh realized she'd have a tough time making a living as a full-time furniture maker. So on her return to Glasgow, she landed a job as an office manager for a custom furniture-making business. She put to use the skills she had developed previously as an executive personal assistant but this time in a creative environment where she had access to a talented designer and a great workshop. Sadly, she reports, the economic climate and financial necessity eventually forced a return to the corporate world. At least for the time being. ∎

SHAPING THE SIDES

Thick slabs of white ash act as bookends for this hall chest, but the gentle contour saves it from seeming heavy, and the polished end grain adds texture.

The ends are formed by thick pieces of ash whose contours are given their rough shape on a bandsaw before they're glued up *(photo 1)*. After that, Kinniburgh gave them their final shape by planing across the grain with a No. 5 jack plane and a No. 4 smoothing plane before finishing with a card scraper and sandpaper *(photo 2)*.

SIDE

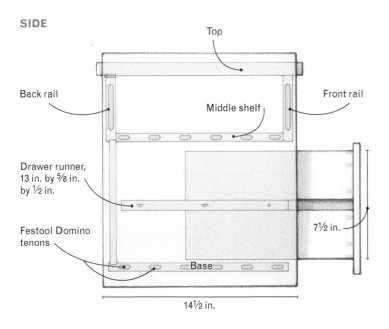

Top

Back rail

Front rail

Middle shelf

Drawer runner, 13 in. by ⅝ in. by ½ in.

Festool Domino tenons

Base

7½ in.

14½ in.

Wood That Flows

Using grain to beckon the eye

PETER TURNER
South Portland, Maine

DIMENSIONS	MATERIALS	HARDWARE	FINISH
48 in. by 16 in. (top); 18 in. high	Hickory, ash	Brass eyelets and nylon rope for lid stays	Shellac (inside); tung oil, varnish, and thinner (outside)

Before Peter Turner designed this chest, he knew he wanted the eye to flow around it. Its curved and rounded edges, along with the bold grain of its ash panels, invite the eye to move, and it's this movement that gives the chest its life.

Peter's 2-year-old godson Ryan was the inspiration behind this element of the design. Ryan got a shiner from an encounter with a table corner, which convinced Peter to eliminate any sharp corners on the lid and make the ends curved instead. Along with the curves at the feet and at the tops of the legs, the top invites the viewer to follow the outlines of the chest all the way around. The simple, flush faces offer nothing to interrupt the eye. Each component seems to have a directional orientation suggesting motion. Because the overall form is quiet, the grain of the wood can speak up.

For the past couple years, Peter has been trying to build only with wood species costing less than $4 a board foot, which is what led him to ash. Peter had no experience with hickory, but was curious about its working characteristics so he chose it for the frames, thinking the two woods would complement one another.

Peter knew from the start that he wanted to use grain to suggest motion, and he let that guide him as he went through stacks of lumber and chose the pieces he needed. Peter found some wide planks that had straight, almost quartered grain along both edges with directional arrows in the flatsawn centers. The grain of the ash panels, cut sequentially from the same plank, forms arrows as it marches across each face of the chest.

Although the four outside faces of the chest are flat, they taper inward at a 3-degree angle from bottom to top. The corner pieces are square to the inside, but are tapered at the same angle on the outside.

To allow the straight grain of the legs to parallel their angled, outer edges, Peter tapered each leg by removing a wedge from the inner edge. In the panels and each frame part, he tried to keep any noticeable grain centered and parallel to an edge.

Frame members are made from 1-in.-thick pieces connected by double floating tenons at each joint; mortises were cut with a router and jig. The bottom of the chest and all four sides are frame-and-panel sections. Inside a storage tray can be slid from side to side on runners let into the top rails.

The grain in all the panels runs parallel to the one-piece top to emphasize the length and stance of the chest. The horizontal, sequential pattern moves from one panel to the next and around the corner from one face to the next. Peter met his goal of the chest having "movement": When he looks at this chest it's hard for his eyes to not want to explore. ▪

OPPOSITE The bold grain of the ash panels in this chest are intended to help the eye move around the piece. Frame pieces are made from hickory.

Wood That Flows

Peter Turner's chest relies on straightforward frame-and-panel construction that showcases white ash panels cut so the grain flows continuously from one section to the next.

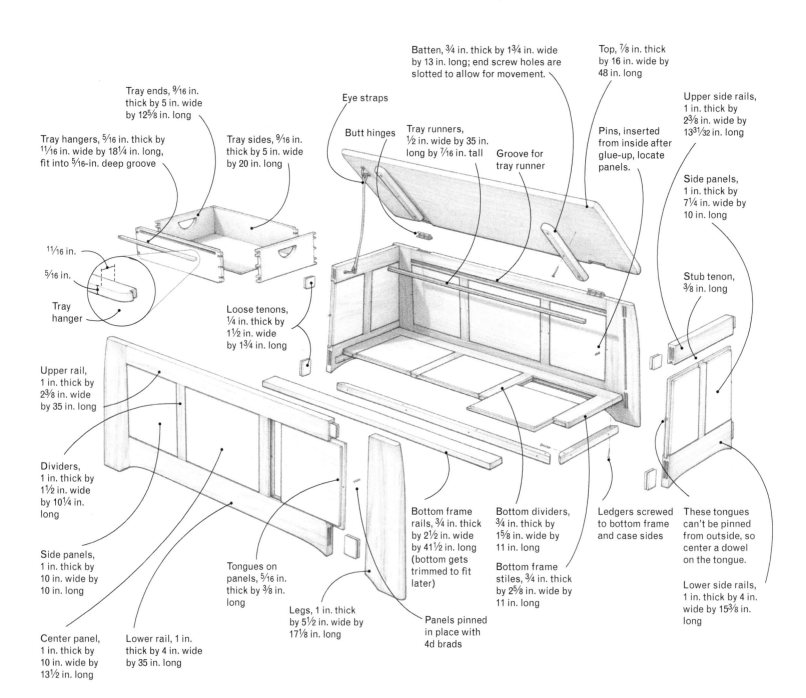

Tray ends, ⁹⁄₁₆ in. thick by 5 in. wide by 12⁵⁄₈ in. long

Tray hangers, ⁵⁄₁₆ in. thick by ¹¹⁄₁₆ in. wide by 18¼ in. long, fit into ⁵⁄₁₆-in. deep groove

Tray sides, ⁹⁄₁₆ in. thick by 5 in. wide by 20 in. long

Eye straps

Butt hinges

Batten, ¾ in. thick by 1¾ in. wide by 13 in. long; end screw holes are slotted to allow for movement.

Tray runners, ½ in. wide by 35 in. long by ⁷⁄₁₆ in. tall

Groove for tray runner

Top, ⁷⁄₈ in. thick by 16 in. wide by 48 in. long

Pins, inserted from inside after glue-up, locate panels.

Upper side rails, 1 in. thick by 2³⁄₈ in. wide by 13³¹⁄₃₂ in. long

Side panels, 1 in. thick by 7¼ in. wide by 10 in. long

11⁄16 in.

5⁄16 in.

Tray hanger

Stub tenon, ³⁄₈ in. long

Loose tenons, ¼ in. thick by 1½ in. wide by 1¾ in. long

Upper rail, 1 in. thick by 2³⁄₈ in. wide by 35 in. long

Dividers, 1 in. thick by 1½ in. wide by 10¼ in. long

Side panels, 1 in. thick by 10 in. wide by 10 in. long

Center panel, 1 in. thick by 10 in. wide by 13½ in. long

Lower rail, 1 in. thick by 4 in. wide by 35 in. long

Tongues on panels, ⁵⁄₁₆ in. thick by ³⁄₈ in. long

Legs, 1 in. thick by 5½ in. wide by 17⅛ in. long

Bottom frame rails, ¾ in. thick by 2½ in. wide by 41½ in. long (bottom gets trimmed to fit later)

Panels pinned in place with 4d brads

Bottom dividers, ¾ in. thick by 1⁵⁄₈ in. wide by 11 in. long

Bottom frame stiles, ¾ in. thick by 2⁵⁄₈ in. wide by 11 in. long

Ledgers screwed to bottom frame and case sides

These tongues can't be pinned from outside, so center a dowel on the tongue.

Lower side rails, 1 in. thick by 4 in. wide by 15³⁄₈ in. long

FRONT

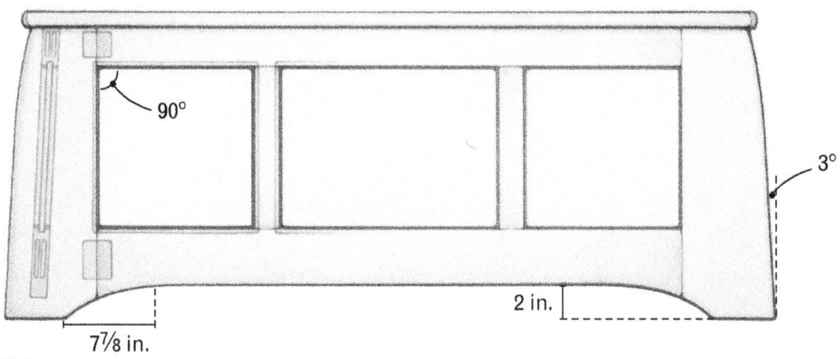

90°

3°

7⅞ in.

2 in.

TOP

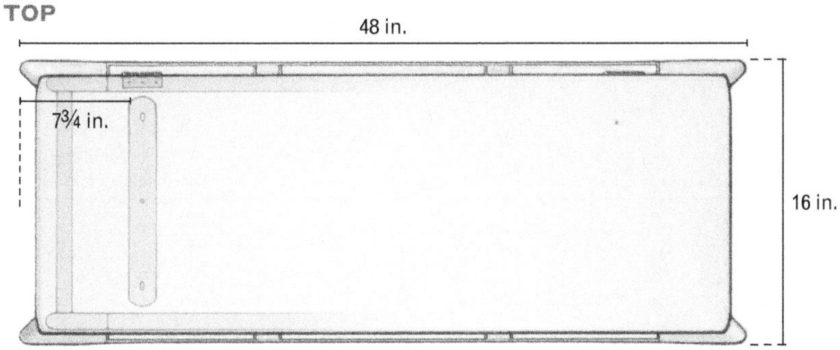

48 in.

7¾ in.

16 in.

SIDE

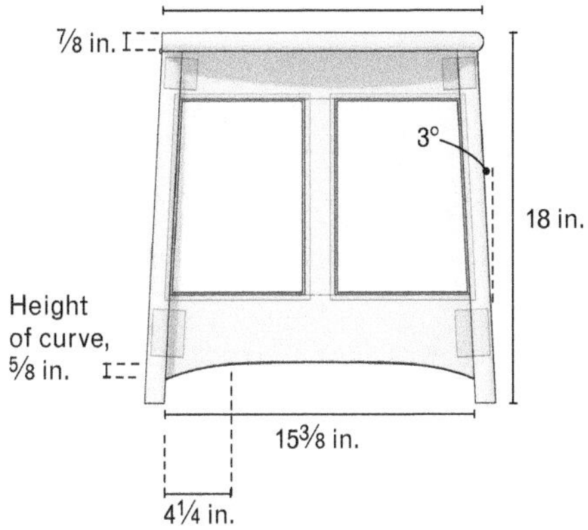

16 in.

⅞ in.

3°

18 in.

Height of curve, ⅝ in.

15⅜ in.

4¼ in.

Taper the Legs First

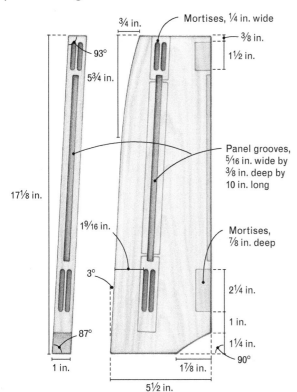

¾ in.

Mortises, ¼ in. wide

⅜ in.

1½ in.

93°

5¾ in.

17⅛ in.

Panel grooves, 5/16 in. wide by ⅜ in. deep by 10 in. long

1 9/16 in.

Mortises, ⅞ in. deep

3°

2¼ in.

1 in.

1¼ in.

87°

90°

1 in.

1⅞ in.

5½ in.

Tapered Sides Reduce Bulk

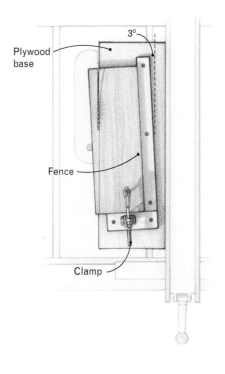

3°

Plywood base

Fence

Clamp

BATTENS KEEP THE LID FLAT

The battens Peter Turner applied to the inside of the chest lid help keep the lid from cupping. Because the grain of the batten runs perpendicular to that of the top, the two pieces of wood must be able to move in relation to each other. Otherwise, the lid might crack.

Each batten is attached to the lid with three screws, one in the middle and one near each end. There need be no allowance for movement at the center of the batten. But at the ends, screws pass through slots so the lid can move with changes in humidity.

A neat way of doing this is by using elongated washers sold by Lee Valley®. They are recessed into the face of the batten so the head of the screw is slightly below the face of the batten after installation.

Start by finding and marking the center point of the batten (photo 1) and laying out the location of a recess at each end (photo 2). These slots should be held back from the end of the batten by about 1 in. The washers are ½ in. wide by 1 in. long, so that's the size the recess will be.

1. Find and mark the center of the batten.

2. Lay out the recesses for the washers.

3. Make the first recess with a plunge router or equivalent tool.

4. Cut a slot of a smaller diameter all the way through the batten.

Turner uses his Multi-Router to make the recesses, but they also can be made with a plunge router with a ½-in. bit *(photo 3)*.

After the recess for the washer is cut, a second slot is made that goes all the way through the batten. The slot is not quite as long as the recess. Turner also cuts this on the Multi-Router, but once again a plunge router will work just as well *(photo 4)*. The result is a recess for the washer plus a slot that runs all the way through the batten *(photo 5)*.

Now bore the screw hole at the center of the batten. The diameter should be slightly larger than the shank of the screw *(photo 6)*.

Choose screw lengths carefully to make sure they don't pop out through the top *(photo 7)*. Remember to allow clearance inside the case for the battens so they won't interfere with an internal tray and to size them so they won't strike the top edges of the box.

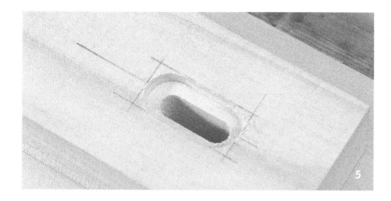

5. The recess provides a shoulder for the washer.

6. Bore a hole at the center of the batten.

7. Make sure the screw length is appropriate for the batten and lid thickness.

Treasure Chest

Stretching a small supply of yew

CHRIS WONG
Port Moody, British Columbia, Canada

DIMENSIONS
21 in. deep, 36 in. wide,
17⅜ in. high

MATERIALS
Pacific yew

HARDWARE
Custom steel-strap hinges,
cut nails

FINISH
Orange shellac

With its rounded top and stout hinges this chest would look right at home on the deck of a privateer's sailing ship. That's no coincidence. Its design sprang from a "classic pirate's treasure chest" Chris Wong built some years ago for fun.

"I was and still am thrilled with how the first chest turned out," he says, "and I'd always wanted to build a large-scale version. With a good idea of the proportions, I just began building and made design decisions on the fly."

Wong made the chest from a very limited supply of Pacific yew he had on hand. "I had to carefully choose how I would use each board," he says. "I began the build by selecting the best, widest pieces for the front of the chest, then for the sides and back. I was left with narrower stock for the lid, which suits the coopered top just fine."

He decided it would be a waste of material to cut away all of the waney edges of the boards and instead decided to leave some to add character. The gap in the top between two live edges forms a natural handle and is one of Wong's favorite details.

The strap hinges are handmade. Wong started with a length of 1½-in.-wide steel strapping. He pounded one end around a ¼-in. steel rod with a heavy ball-peen hammer, and then cut knuckles into mating pieces to form a hinge. A length of ¼-in. steel rod makes each pin, the ends peened over to lock them in place.

To match the hinges to the contours of the box, Wong placed the straps between two metal bench dogs and bent them to the correct shape. Then he bored 3/16-in. holes through the steel and sprayed the hinges with black paint. They're attached to the chest with cut nails cinched over on the inside. In hindsight, Wong realizes that objects stored inside the chest could become snagged on a nail and thinks screws might have been a better choice.

The sides of the chest taper outward slightly, increasing an inch overall in both width and depth from the floor to the top of the lid. The bottom is a raised panel let into a groove near the bottom of the chest sides. By the time he got to that point his supply of lumber was nearly spent; the bottom is actually made from 17 pieces glued up in brick-laid fashion.

"I did not know how it would look when it was finished," he says. "As with many projects, I start with just an idea of what I want it to look like when I am done, and it continues to evolve as the build progresses. Often, people will ask me what I am making and my answer is, 'I'll let you know.'"

Treasure Chest

This chest by Chris Wong is joined with through dovetails. The rounded top is coopered, and the strap hinges custom made.

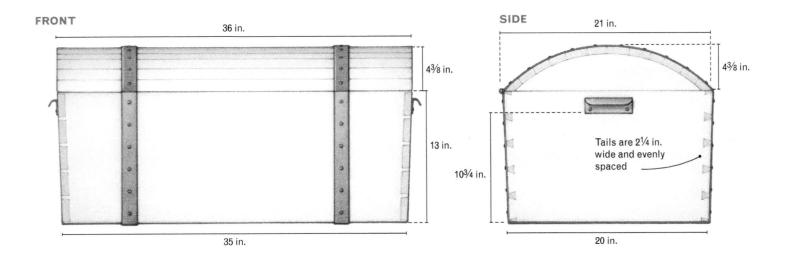

FRONT

36 in.

4³⁄₈ in.

13 in.

35 in.

SIDE

21 in.

4³⁄₈ in.

10³⁄₄ in.

Tails are 2¹⁄₄ in. wide and evenly spaced

20 in.

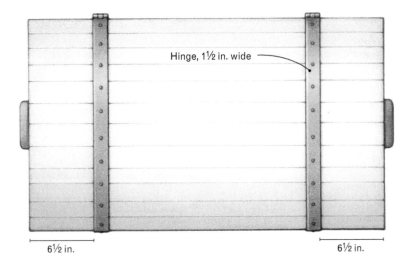

TOP

Hinge, 1½ in. wide

6½ in.

6½ in.

DETAIL OF HINGE

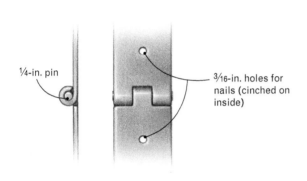

¼-in. pin

³⁄₁₆-in. holes for nails (cinched on inside)

DETAIL OF HANDLE

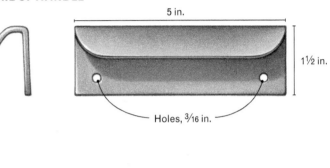

5 in.

1½ in.

Holes, ³⁄₁₆ in.

DETAIL OF BOTTOM

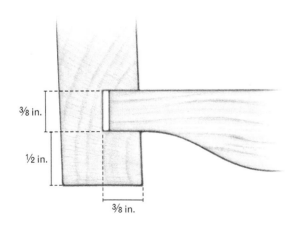

⅜ in.

½ in.

⅜ in.

Simply Proportions

Using wood that speaks softly

LIZA WHEELER
Belfast, Maine

DIMENSIONS	MATERIALS	HARDWARE	FINISH
19⅝ in. deep, 39½ in. wide, 25⅝ in. high	Douglas fir, western red cedar	Brass butt hinges (oxidized with potassium dichromate), folding iron lid stay	Wax

iza Wheeler's work is often directed by wood she comes across. Rather than develop a design first and then hope she can find the lumber to make it work, Wheeler lets the particular personality of the wood take the lead. And in this case, Douglas fir pointed the way. "I was enamored of Douglas fir and its quiet, linear grain," Wheeler says. "When I saw this wood, I thought of an expanse of fir with only the joinery interrupting those grain lines."

"When you build out of a softwood, the wood reveals the touch of your hand," she adds. "It's almost as though it comes from under the plane already having a patina. Cutting clean dovetail joints in softwood, especially a splintery wood like fir, is trickier than you might think. I had to keep the tools sharp."

Wheeler says the lid was meant to be a continuation of the sides of the chest, but she realized there had to be some separation between them. She introduced a 1/8-in. gap between the chest and the lid by rabbeting a rectangular piece of molding into the case to give the lid a positive stop. At the bottom of the chest is a 5/16-in. shadow line.

The lid incorporates panels that Wheeler thinks in hindsight are too delicate to serve as a seat. She would rather have made the lid strong enough to handle "whatever may come its way," but the panels are as thick as the material would allow, and Wheeler made the case a little taller than it might otherwise have been to discourage people from sitting on it.

Inside the chest are storage trays made from red cedar. The corners are rabbeted and pinned, and the surface left with a hand-planed finish. For their use, she says, the trays need joinery no more elaborate than that.

Wheeler says she always makes full-scale drawings of a piece, and in this case did a mockup of the box in cardboard to see what the dimensions would look like. Because the dovetails at the corners of the case are just about the only added detail, success hinged totally on proportion.

Wheeler cites James Krenov as a favorite designer and maker, praising his "use of proportion, wood selection, and understated detailing." Wheeler studied woodworking at Seattle Central Community College in Seattle, Washington, in 1992 and 1993.

"I learned from this project and many others," Wheeler says, "that the furniture that speaks to me has a simplicity that belies the difficulty of creating it." ▪

OPPOSITE Liza Wheeler's chest in Douglas fir has virtually no surface decoration, relying on proportion and the wood itself to make the design work.

ABOVE Rectangular molding set into a rabbet in the sides of the chest maintain a 1/8-in. gap between the case and lid.

Simply Proportions

The intrinsic beauty of Douglas fir helped shape the design of this chest. Its only real ornamentation is the through dovetails that join the case. Inside, storage trays have a pinned and rabbeted butt joint.

TOP

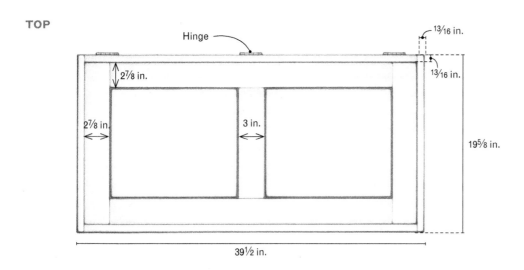

Hinge

$\frac{13}{16}$ in.

$\frac{13}{16}$ in.

$2\frac{7}{8}$ in.

$2\frac{7}{8}$ in.

3 in.

$19\frac{5}{8}$ in.

$39\frac{1}{2}$ in.

FRONT   **SIDE**

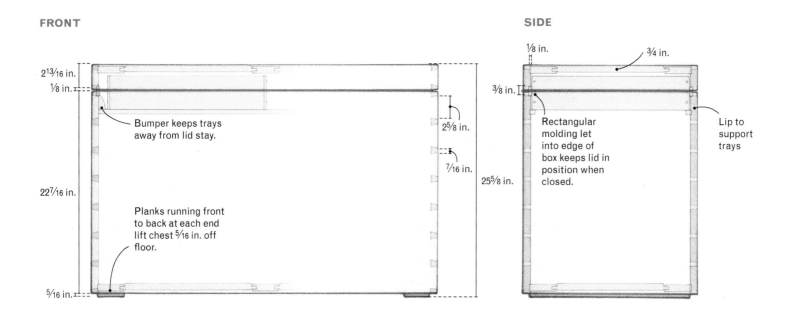

$2\frac{13}{16}$ in.

$\frac{1}{8}$ in.

Bumper keeps trays away from lid stay.

$22\frac{7}{16}$ in.

Planks running front to back at each end lift chest $\frac{5}{16}$ in. off floor.

$\frac{5}{16}$ in.

$2\frac{5}{8}$ in.

$\frac{7}{16}$ in.

$25\frac{5}{8}$ in.

$\frac{1}{8}$ in.

$\frac{3}{4}$ in.

$\frac{3}{8}$ in.

Rectangular molding let into edge of box keeps lid in position when closed.

Lip to support trays

TRAY DETAIL

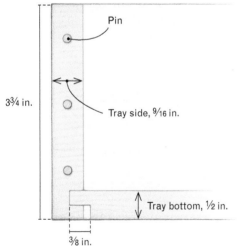

Pin

Tray side, 9/16 in.

3¾ in.

Tray bottom, ½ in.

⅜ in.

Given the material she had to work with, the panels in the lid are not as robust as Wheeler would have liked, so she made the chest more than 25 in. high to discourage its use as a bench. Trays inside are made from western red cedar, rabbeted and pinned at the corners.

Box of Blue

Details add a rich visual layer to a simple box

GARRETT HACK
Thetford Center, Vermont

DIMENSIONS
18 in. deep, 43½ in. wide, 21 in. high

MATERIALS
Butternut, inlays of holly and ebony, faux lapis lazuli panels (paint and gold powder), rosewood moldings, white cedar bottom

HARDWARE
Brass hinges

FINISH
Tinted shellac, thinned varnish, wax

Like many furniture makers with their roots in New England, Garrett Hack was influenced early in his career by Shaker designs. The restored Shaker village in Canterbury, New Hampshire, was close enough for frequent visits, and Hack could get a firsthand look at its architecture, woodwork, and furniture.

But as his skills developed, Hack turned to a more diverse library of styles, and he went on to study work of the Federal period in southern New England and the Mid-Atlantic states. The Federal style emerged after the Revolutionary War as craftsmen looked for a distinctly American imprint. It was characterized by a lightness of design, curved or elliptical features, and finely wrought details.

Both of those influences seem apparent in Hack's *Box of Blue*. Its Shaker-like case is butternut, a classic American hardwood, joined at its corners with neat rows of exposed dovetails. "The construction is simple, very effective, and quick," Hack says. "Plus, everyone loves to see dovetails."

It is the details, however, that widen the chest's vocabulary to something more complex than Shaker. First, there is the base. Beginning at the interior edge of the foot, it arches gently toward the middle, where it takes another turn to dip into an arc at the center set off with an inlaid edge of black and white.

The narrow breadboard ends on the lid are set off with a strip of the same ebony and holly inlay used to highlight the center of the base. Across the front of the chest are small inlaid squares of ebony. A till (a small inner box) inside the chest also is detailed with a dot-dash line of inlay along its lid.

But the most compelling detail is the slight recesses on the lid and front of the case that have been painted to look like lapis lazuli, a semiprecious stone with an intense blue color. Hack thought lapis seemed to be in "good harmony" with the color of the butternut, but the recessed panels were among the most difficult parts of the design to work out.

Hack used a router to rough out the recesses, then pared them back to a clean line with a chisel. Because the bottom of the recess would be painted to look like polished stone, the surface had to be dead flat, and that was no small feat. Further, it wasn't possible for Hack's wife, Carolyn, to paint cleanly all the way into each corner, so Hack added tiny pieces of rosewood molding to hide the transition. The color is a blend of paint and gold powder.

(CONTINUED)

For all of the intricacies of design, Hack's approach is relatively low key. He started with some sketches, went to a scaled drawing, and then got to work. There were no models and no prototypes, and some things changed as he went. Hack refined the size of the foot, for example, to make the chest slightly higher. The size and layout of the faux lapis panels wasn't determined until the chest had been assembled. The dot-dash line on the till inside was done by eye, not with a template.

All of it worked, especially the faux painting. "It gave me the confidence to try other faux work," he says. "My wife is a painter and can paint anything. Since then, Carolyn and I have done malachite panels and verde antique columns, and we have a piece going now with a combination of many painting details." ■

ABOVE Inside the chest is a small till for keeping special things. Its lid is adorned with edging of ebony and holly laid out by eye.

RIGHT The signature detail of Hack's chest is the recessed panels painted to look like polished stone. Recesses were made with a router and refined with a card scraper.

Box of Blue

Garrett Hack's butternut chest combines classic elements, such as breadboard ends on the lid and exposed dovetail joinery on the case, with decorative details that include recesses painted to resemble polished stone.

TOP

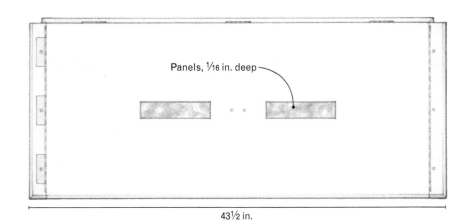

Panels, 1/16 in. deep

43½ in.

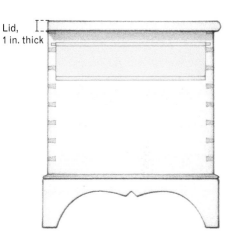

Lid, 1 in. thick

FRONT

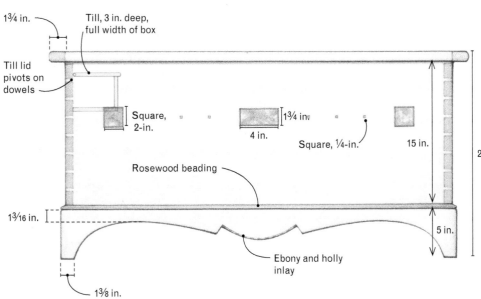

1¾ in.

Till, 3 in. deep, full width of box

Till lid pivots on dowels

Square, 2-in.

4 in.

1¾ in.

Square, ¼-in.

15 in.

21 in.

Rosewood beading

1 3/16 in.

5 in.

Ebony and holly inlay

1⅜ in.

DETAIL OF BASE CONNECTION

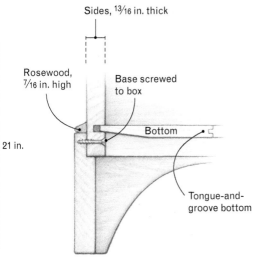

Sides, 13/16 in. thick

Rosewood, 7/16 in. high

Base screwed to box

Bottom

Tongue-and-groove bottom

Chest as Storyteller

Carved panels draw on rich traditions of Chinese art

JEFFREY COOPER
Portsmouth, New Hampshire

DIMENSIONS
33 in. wide, 22 in. deep,
19½ in. high.

MATERIALS
Cherry

HARDWARE
SOSS® invisible hinges, brass
lid support

FINISH
Catalyzed lacquer

Jeffrey Cooper had in mind a locker-style chest that could be set at the foot of a bed and used for blankets and bedding or, alternately, placed between a couple of chairs in the living room and used as a coffee table. Whatever its final destination, its focal point could be nothing but the four carved panels that together make up the sides of the chest.

The carvings are based on paintings at the Beijing Museum of Art, including a 12th-century illustration of a poem written by Emperor Su Shih. The title for the chest, *The Purple Cliffs and other stories,* is derived from that painting; carvings on the other three panels are based on work by three different artists.

Cooper's furniture has long included carved elements. But on a trip to China, he became intrigued with the narrative quality of the art he saw. He began experimenting with those themes and produced a number of wall hangings. A Chinese stool he saw at the Boston Museum of Fine Arts gave him an idea for incorporating his ideas in chest form.

Cooper worked from scaled construction drawings and full-size drawings for the carved panels. The panels are relief carvings, meaning that elements of the composition take shape as material around them is removed. He started with 5/4 material, milled to a thickness of 1 in., to guarantee he'd have enough material to work with.

Frame-and-panel construction was really Cooper's only choice for assembly. But instead of a conventional design in which rectangular frames are joined with right-angle corners, Cooper chose solid corner posts. In some ways, the posts simplified design, and they also allowed him to shape the corners without cutting into any joinery.

The three-way mitered corners seem apt from a design standpoint because they're common in Chinese furniture. But Cooper knew from experience they could be challenging, and it prompted him to buy himself his first chopsaw ("How did I live without it?" he now asks).

Trying to glue the entire chest together at one time would have been a nightmare. Cooper knew that from experience. He had used the three-way miter on a table while in school and had started to glue up everything at once. A passing comment from an instructor walking by convinced him to pull it apart while he could and approach the glue-up in stages.

(CONTINUED)

OPPOSITE Jeffrey Cooper thought this chest could be used as a coffee table as easily as a blanket chest. Its design is dominated by four carved panels, each an interpretation of paintings he saw in China.

ABOVE Starting with a 1-in.-thick cherry panel gave Cooper enough meat for the relief carvings. This one comes from *Eagle on a Maple Tree* by Hua Yen, whose work spanned the 17th and 18th centuries.

And that's how he tackled the chest. When all of the parts had been shaped and fitted, he assembled the whole chest but glued only those parts on the ends. When the glue in those sections set, he took the chest apart, made any necessary adjustments in the remaining pieces, and then put it all back together—this time with glue for the side assemblies. Cooper glued blocks to the corner posts for clamps and cut them away later.

Although he wanted the top to be of substantial thickness, Cooper also wanted to keep the weight down. He used a type of hollow-core construction, starting with a stapled lattice of 3/8-in.-thick poplar pieces 3/4 in. wide. That's covered with 3/8-in. MDF and then with 1/32-in. cherry veneer. In addition to being much lighter than a solid top, this one also is more stable dimensionally. Inside is a lift-out tray that sits in notches cut into the corner posts.

Cooper used SOSS concealed hinges, so with the lid closed nothing interferes with the carvings and the stories they tell. ■

This panel is fashioned after "Flowers," a work by 19th-century Chinese artist Chi-Chien.

Triple Miter Corners

The 2¾-in.-square corner posts were milled from 12/4 stock and notched on the inside for a pull-out tray. The triple miter joint is splined for added strength.

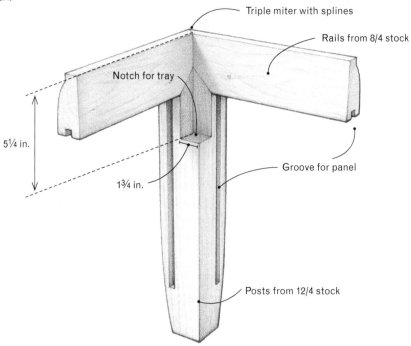

Triple miter with splines

Rails from 8/4 stock

Notch for tray

Groove for panel

5¼ in.

1¾ in.

Posts from 12/4 stock

Chest as Storyteller

Jeffrey Cooper's cherry chest is of frame-and-panel construction with solid corner posts and a hollow-core top.

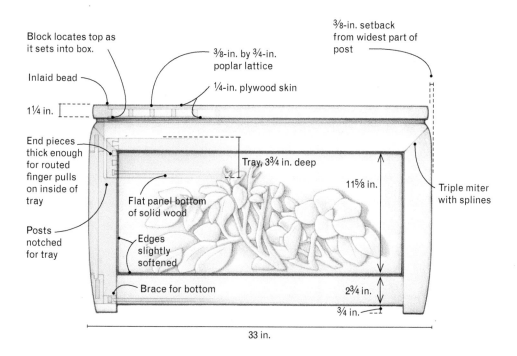

Block locates top as it sets into box.

⅜-in. by ¾-in. poplar lattice

⅜-in. setback from widest part of post

Inlaid bead

¼-in. plywood skin

1¼ in.

End pieces thick enough for routed finger pulls on inside of tray

Tray, 3¾ in. deep

11⅝ in.

Triple miter with splines

Flat panel bottom of solid wood

Posts notched for tray

Edges slightly softened

Brace for bottom

2¾ in.

¾ in.

33 in.

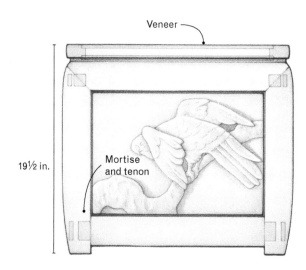

Veneer

19½ in.

Mortise and tenon

Unexpected Details

Color and contrasting shapes lend a contemporary flavor

CAROL BASS
Yarmouth, Maine

DIMENSIONS	MATERIALS	HARDWARE	FINISH
18 in. deep, 43 in. wide, 28½ in. high	Hard maple, nylon rope (lid stay)	1½-in. by 2½-in. butt hinges, 2-in. bronze eyes	Oil-based stains, conversion varnish

A n appreciation for clean, contemporary shapes and playful color helped steer Carol Bass as she designed this blanket chest for a master bedroom. It was built by Peter Turner of South Portland, Maine (for a look at Turner's ash and hickory chest, see p. 136).

Anyone familiar with Maine Cottage Furniture will know something about Bass's design sense. The Yarmouth-based company, which she started with her former husband in 1988, sells a line of furniture and accessories often finished in bright colors. Bass, in fact, is an artist and painter as well as a designer. She got the idea for the company when she couldn't find furniture for her own home that didn't clash or take away from her collection of contemporary Maine paintings and sculpture. The company now operates retail stores in Maine, South Carolina, and Florida and says 90 percent of its custom-made and finished pieces are built in New England or North Carolina shops.

Although the overall shape of this chest is traditional for a blanket chest, many of the details are not. That includes the angled top, the oversize double ball feet, and the ends of the case, which are really large frame-and-panel assemblies. The translucent wash of color over the maple case is a combination of one coat each of blue and green oil-based stain.

Bass says the idea for the form as well as the color came from a ceramic piece in the corner of the room for which the chest was designed. She finds the result "gentle and humorous and subtle." She cites a variety of makers and styles as influential, including Isamu Noguchi, Hans Wegner, Ernest Race, Shaker, Mission, and primitive arts.

Turner says the idea of having dovetails at the top and bottom of the case, rather than all the way down each corner, was part of Bass's initial sketch. He introduced rails at the top and bottom of the chest ends, and housed the panels in dados cut into the inside of the case. The panels are pinned to keep them centered.

The centerlines of the dovetails in both the lid and the case are parallel to each other (and to the floor). One reason for choosing this approach for the angled lid, Turner says, was to avoid short-grain strength issues that would have resulted with dovetail centerlines perpendicular to the lid's edge.

(CONTINUED)

OPPOSITE Carol Bass designed this chest with an angular lid and a wash of blue-green after seeing a piece of ceramic at the client's home. It was built by Peter Turner.

ABOVE Stacked spheres of clear finished maple contrast with the angular lines of the chest. They are connected to the chest with tenons.

The top also is of frame-and-panel construction. If he were to make the chest again, Turner says he would consider reducing panel thickness to ½ in. to reduce the weight of the top.

The angled lid did make the glue-up a little tricky, but Turner says angled clamping pads available for his Bessey® K-body clamps helped and made separate cauls unnecessary.

Turner drew scaled drawings from the sketch that Bass provided and built the chest from those. Because the design was straightforward, he did not make a prototype. "The design grew on me," he says. "I liked the way it looked more and more as the project went along." ▪

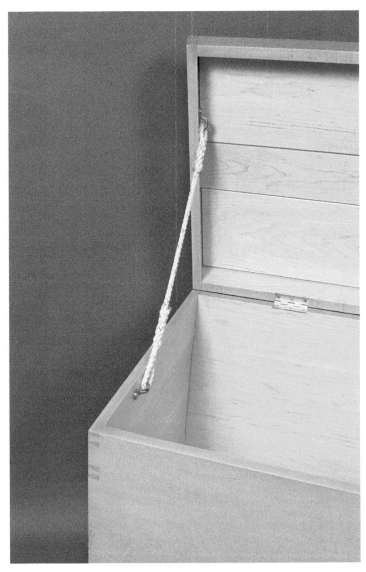

ABOVE The sides and lid of the chest are angled in one dimension but flat on the front and back.

RIGHT The lid stay is a simple piece of nylon rope with a splice woven into each end and attached to brass hardware.

Unexpected Details

Carol Bass gave this chest the same design spirit she put into Maine Cottage Furniture, including contemporary shapes and lively color. Its frame-and-panel and dovetail construction are solidly traditional.

TOP

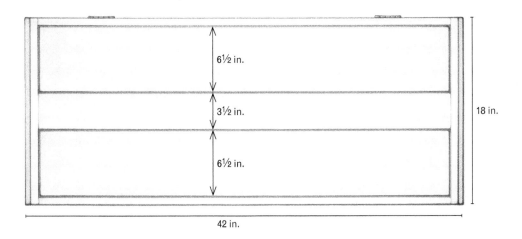

FRONT

SIDE

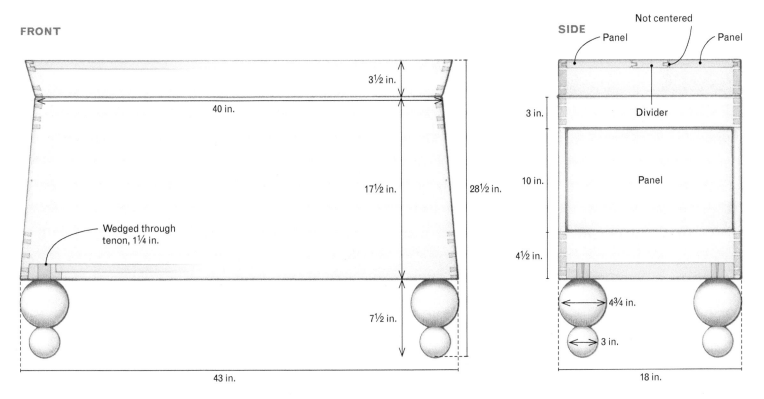

CUTTING ANGLED DOVETAILS

The dovetailed lid of the blanket chest designed by Carol Bass and built by Peter Turner is angled outward on the sides, whereas the front and back of the lid are straight up and down. This means the ends of the front and back pieces of the lid are cut at an angle and the ends of the side pieces are at 90 degrees.

Cutting angled dovetails is not much different than cutting through dovetails on a square corner, but they are laid out differently. Instead of the centerline of the dovetails being perpendicular to the angled edge, they are parallel to the top and bottom edges of the lid to prevent weak short-grain in the joint.

In these photos, the pins are cut into the side pieces of the lid; the tails are cut in the front and back pieces. Don't forget that the top and bottom edges of the side pieces must be beveled. Stock for the side pieces consequently must be a little wider to start. In other respects, this process is very straightforward. (You'll find a more detailed explanation of cutting dovetails in Chest-Building Techniques, beginning on p. 5).

Using a marking gauge set to the thickness of the side pieces, cut a line in the angled ends of the front and back pieces of the lid *(photo 1)*.

1. With a marking gauge set to the thickness of the side pieces, mark a baseline at both ends of the front and back of the lid.

2. Centerlines for the sockets are parallel to the top and bottom edges.

3. Mark the width of the sockets at each end.

4. Set a bevel gauge to correspond with the layout line on one side of the socket.

Mark the centerlines of the tail sockets with a square, using the top and bottom edges of the piece as the reference *(photo 2)*. The centerlines should be parallel to the top and bottom.

With a ruler, mark the dimensions of both ends of the tail socket *(photo 3)*. The sockets will be wider on the inside of the lid than out near the edge. To get these dimensions, measure another dovetail or lay one out on a piece of scrap.

Use the marks to set a bevel gauge and then use the gauge to mark one side of the sockets *(photo 4)*. Because the centerlines are not perpendicular to the edge, angles for the two sides of the dovetail are different. You'll need a second gauge to set the other angle.

Use a second gauge to find the other angle. Then mark this line as needed to complete the layout of the tail sockets all the way around the lid *(photo 5)*.

Color the area to be removed to help you avoid making a mistake *(photo 6)*. Then saw out the sockets, remove the waste, and use the tail pieces to mark pins on the side pieces.

5. Use a second bevel gauge to set the second side of the socket and complete the layout.

6. Filling in the area to be removed with a colored pencil helps avoid mistakes.

A Pair of Oak Chests

Understated design holds several surprises

STEPHEN LAMONT
Alton, Hampshire, United Kingdom

DIMENSIONS
24 in. deep, 48 in. wide,
29 in. high

MATERIALS
European oak, black walnut,
cedar of Lebanon

HARDWARE
Extruded brass hinges with
shopmade reinforcing plates,
hidden full-extension drawer
slides

FINISH
Wax

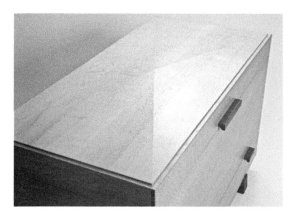

Some of the most interesting details in this chest by Stephen Lamont may not be apparent on first glance. There is the faceted top, for example, the double-lapped dovetails, and the custom hinges that also serve as stops for the lid.

In its overall presentation, however, the chest, one of a pair built at the same time, speaks to Lamont's training with Devon furniture maker Christopher Faulkner, his study and eventual stint as a teacher and craftsman at the Edward Barnsley Workshop, and his overall debt of gratitude to the British Arts and Crafts movement.

Lamont is a one-time professional pilot from the United States who switched to furniture making. After studying under Faulkner, he returned to work in Pennsylvania for a number of years and eventually resettled to England, where he now works in shared shop space in Alton, about midway between London and Portsmouth on England's southern coast.

The identical chests each have a pair of 6-in.-deep drawers plus a main storage compartment for bulky items, such as blankets, duvets, and the like. They are lined with cedar, a natural insect repellent.

Both are made from one tree of European oak. Lamont bought the whole tree, which had been sawn into planks and kiln dried. The sturdy bases that lift the chests off the floor are made from black walnut.

Lamont's favorite design feature is the double-lapped dovetails for the case. These are similar to half-blind dovetails that are typically used for a drawer except they're cut into a rabbet. When the joint is assembled, all evidence of the dovetails is hidden. What shows on the outside of the case is a thin stripe of end grain. The technique offers the robust mechanical connection of dovetails, and also allowed Lamont to solve a key design puzzle: how to hide the short edges of end grain on the drawer fronts (see Making a Double-Lap Dovetail Joint on pp. 18–21 for more on this technique).

From a distance, the lids of the chests could look flat. But in reality, they are planed to form four triangular sections that rise gradually to meet at a point in the center of the lid. The outermost edges are 5mm thick, increasing to the full 18mm thickness (roughly ¾ in.) over the course of the taper. In making the lids, Lamont started with material roughly 2 in. thick, drew the diagonals to get the center

(CONTINUED)

point, and then marked the depth of the facet around the edge. He used a scrub plane and then a jack plane to form the faces.

The lid and its sides are joined in what Lamont calls an F-joint that allows the lumber to move seasonally with changes in humidity. In the years since he built the chests, Lamont says he's noticed the lids have shrunk slightly, but they've put no strain on the joinery in the remainder of the top.

Finally, there are the hinges. Rather than install a stay inside the chest, Lamont decided to keep the interior clean, so he modified butt hinges to provide their own stops. He soldered extra plates to both leaves of the hinges, each with a beveled edge along its long axis. When the hinge opens, the plates catch the weight. "It was a bit risky with the weight of the tops and the amount of leverage," he says, "but there have been no problems." That was one detail he worked out along the way. ▪

LEFT The case is assembled with a hidden joint called a double-lap dovetail. Neither pins nor tails are visible when the sides of the case are put together.

Lamont soldered extra plates to the leaf hinges to make an integral stop for the lid. When the top is opened just past 90 degrees, the beveled edges of the plates meet and prevent the lid from opening any farther.

The black walnut drawer pulls contrast nicely with the pale oak.

Hinges with Built-In Stops

By soldering beveled reinforcing plates to the leaves of butt hinges, Lamont created hinges with integral stops and eliminated the need to install a separate stay for the lid.

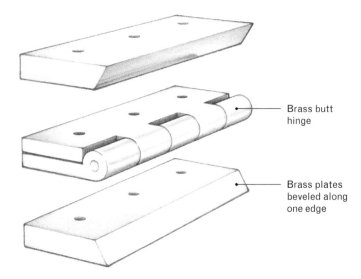

Brass butt hinge

Brass plates beveled along one edge

A Pair of Oak Chests

Stephen Lamont's oak chests are made from a single tree of European oak and joined with hidden double-lap dovetails.

FRONT

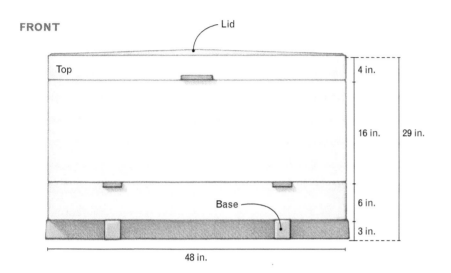

Lid

Top

4 in.

16 in.

29 in.

6 in.

Base

3 in.

48 in.

SIDE

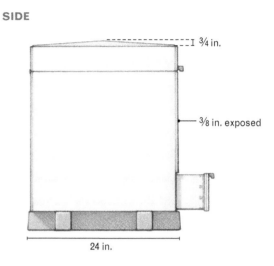

¾ in.

⅜ in. exposed

24 in.

TOP

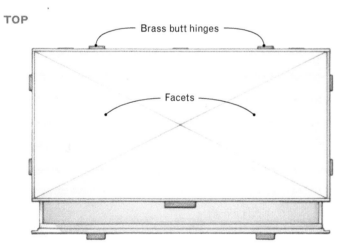

Brass butt hinges

Facets

Lid with an "F Joint"

The lid is attached to the sides of the top with a joint that allows seasonal movement of the lid without pushing against the sides. Gaps are eliminated.

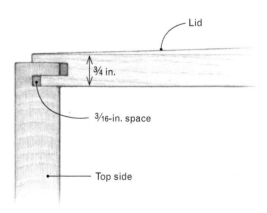

Lid

¾ in.

³⁄₁₆-in. space

Top side

Metric Equivalents

INCHES	CENTIMETERS	MILLIMETERS	INCHES	CENTIMETERS	MILLIMETERS
1/8	0.3	3	13	33.0	330
1/4	0.6	6	14	35.6	356
3/8	1.0	10	15	38.1	381
1/2	1.3	13	16	40.6	406
5/8	1.6	16	17	43.2	432
3/4	1.9	19	18	45.7	457
7/8	2.2	22	19	48.3	483
1	2.5	25	20	50.8	508
1 1/4	3.2	32	21	53.3	533
1 1/2	3.8	38	22	55.9	559
1 3/4	4.4	44	23	58.4	584
2	5.1	51	24	61.0	610
2 1/2	6.4	64	25	63.5	635
3	7.6	76	26	66.0	660
3 1/2	8.9	89	27	68.6	686
4	10.2	102	28	71.1	711
4 1/2	11.4	114	29	73.7	737
5	12.7	127	30	76.2	762
6	15.2	152	31	78.7	787
7	17.8	178	32	81.3	813
8	20.3	203	33	83.8	838
9	22.9	229	34	86.4	864
10	25.4	254	35	88.9	889
11	27.9	279	36	91.4	914
12 1/2	30.5	305			

Contributors

CAROL BASS
Yarmouth, Maine
carolrbass@gmail.com
See Unexpected Details, p. 158

TED BLACHLY
Warner, New Hampshire
t_blachly@mcttelecom.com
See Danika's Chest, p. 96

JEFFREY COOPER
Portsmouth, New Hampshire
jcooper@cooperwoodsculptor.com
See Chest as Storyteller, p. 154

MICHAEL CULLEN
Petaluma, California
michael@michaelcullendesign
See Red Leaf Chest, p. 36

CHARLIE DURFEE
Woolwich, Maine
durfodd@suscom-maine.net
See Curly Cherry Classic, p. 104

BRUCE EATON
Hampton, New Hampshire
bruceeaton@comcast.net
See Cabinetmaking Traditions,
  p. 122

MIGUEL GÓMEZ-IBÁÑEZ
Boston, Massachusetts
president@nbss.edu
See A Wedding Chest, p. 118

GARRETT HACK
Thetford Center, Vermont
abundance.farm@valley.net
See Box of Blue, p. 150

EJLER HJORTH-WESTH
Elk, California
ejler@mcn.org
See A Boat Builder's Chest, p. 88

SHONA KINNIBURGH
Glasgow, Scotland
mail@shona-kinniburgh.co.uk
See Function Meets Elegance,
  p. 132

STEPHEN LAMONT
Hampshire, United Kingdom
stephen.lamont@virgin.net
See A Pair of Oak Chests, p. 164

AUSTIN MATHESON
Rockport, Maine
austin@finehandmadefurniture.
  com
See Bermudan Chest, p. 32

LAURA MAYS
Galway, Ireland
laura@yaffemays.com
See A Chest for Life, p. 48

JOHN MCALEVEY
Warren, Maine
johnmacalevey@gmail.com
See Plain and Simple, p. 42

TERRY MOORE
Wilmot, New Hampshire
terrykmoore@tds.net
See A Chest for Work, p. 72

DARRELL PEART
Seattle, Washington
dwp@furnituremaker.com
See Celebrating Arts and Crafts,
  p. 108

PETER PIEROBON
Vancouver, British Columbia
pierobon3@aol.com
See Little House, p. 76

BRIAN REID
Rockland, Maine
brian@brianreidfurniture.com
See Flower Power, p. 92

MITCH RYERSON
Cambridge, Massachusetts
mitchryerson@yahoo.com
See Sea Chest, p. 80

BRIAN SARGENT
Candia, New Hampshire
blsdesigns126@earthlink.net
See Waterfall Chest, p. 28

LIBBY SCHRUM
Camden, Maine
libbyschrum@gmail.com
See Modern Lines, p. 52

ROBERT SCHULTZ
Kimberly, Wisconsin
rschultz1@new.rr.com
See The Un-Chest, p. 58

GREGORY SMITH
Fort Bragg, California
gsmith@prxy.com
See Chest in the Round, p. 100

DAVID STENSTROM
Portland, Maine
lastchance@maine.rr.com
See Pilgrim Century, p. 128

CRAIG THIBODEAU
San Diego, California
info@ctfinefurniture.com
See Dogwood Blanket Chest, p. 66

PETER TURNER
South Portland, Maine
petersturner@hotmail.com
See Wood That Flows, p. 136

RICHARD VAUGHAN
Queensland, Australia
worksinwood@netspace.net.au
See Chest of Blankets, p. 62

J-P VILKMAN
Helsinki, Finland
j-p@j-pvilkman.com
see Alabama Man, p. 114

LIZA WHEELER
Belfast, Maine
lwheeler1003@gmail.com
See Simply Proportions, p. 146

CHRIS WONG
Port Moody, British Columbia
chris@flairwoodworks.com
See Treasure Chest, p. 142

Photo Credits

PAGE IV Chris Pinchbeck, Pinchbeck Photography

PAGE 2 © Scott Gibson © The Taunton Press, Inc.

PAGES 4-25 © Scott Gibson © The Taunton Press, Inc.

PAGES 28-29 © Bill Truslow

PAGE 31 Brian Sargent

PAGES 32-34 Chris Pinchbeck, Pinchbeck Photography

PAGE 36 Barbara Cullen

PAGE 39 Don Russel

PAGES 40-41 Barbara Cullen

PAGES 42-43 Charley Frieberg

PAGES 46-47 Scott Gibson © The Taunton Press, Inc.

PAGES 43-50 Laura Mays

PAGES 52-54 Chris Pinchbeck, Pinchbeck Photography

PAGES 56-57 Scott Gibson © The Taunton Press, Inc.

PAGES 58-59, 61 Robert A. Schultz

PAGES 62-63 Richard Vaughan

PAGES 66-71 Craig Carlson

PAGES 72-73, 75 Charlie Frieberg

PAGES 76-78 Joe Chielli

PAGE 80 Dean Powell

PAGES 84-87 Scott Gibson © The Taunton Press, Inc.

PAGES 88-89 © Randy O'Rourke

PAGE 91 Kevin O'Shea

PAGES 92-93 Jim Dugan

PAGES 96-98 Scott Gibson © The Taunton Press, Inc

PAGES 100-102 John Birchard

PAGE 104-105 Guy Marsden

PAGES 108-109, 112-113 Darrell Peart

PAGE 110 The Gamble House/USC, Greene and Greene Archives

PAGE 114-115 Jari-Pekka Vilkman

PAGES 118, 120 Dean Powell

PAGES 122-123 Bruce Eaton

PAGE 126-127 Scott Gibson © The Taunton Press, Inc.

PAGE 128 John Tanabe

PAGES 129, 131 Scott Gibson © The Taunton Press Inc.

PAGES 132-133 www.jimdugan.com

PAGE 135 Shona Kinniburgh

PAGE 136 Anissa Kapsales, courtesy *Fine Woodworking* magazine, © The Taunton Press, Inc.

PAGES 142-143 Martin Truax

PAGES 146-147, 149 www.jiimdugan.com

PAGES 150-152 John Sherman

PAGES 154-155 © Bill Truslow

PAGES 156-160, 162-163 Scott Gibson © The Taunton Press, Inc.

PAGES 164-166 Chris Warren Photography, East Meon, Hampshire, United Kingdom

Index

Note: **Bold** page numbers indicate a photo, and *italicized* page numbers indicate a drawing. (When only one number of a page range is **bold** or *italicized*, a photo or illustration appears on one or more of the pages.)